Never Play Dead

Never Play Dead

How the Truth Makes You Unstoppable

TOMI LAHREN

BROADSIDE BOOKS
An Imprint of HarperCollins*Publishers*

NEVER PLAY DEAD. Copyright © 2019 by Tomi Lahren. All rights reserved. Printed in the United States of America. No part of this book may be used or reproduced in any manner whatsoever without written permission except in the case of brief quotations embodied in critical articles and reviews. For information, address HarperCollins Publishers, 195 Broadway, New York, NY 10007.

HarperCollins books may be purchased for educational, business, or sales promotional use. For information, please email the Special Markets Department at SPsales@harpercollins.com.

Broadside Books™ and the Broadside logo are trademarks of HarperCollins Publishers.

FIRST EDITION

Library of Congress Cataloging-in-Publication Data has been applied for.

ISBN 978-0-06-288194-6

19 20 21 22 23   LSC   10 9 8 7 6 5 4 3 2 1

To my mom and dad, for teaching me
what's worth fighting for.

To Brandon, for loving me through it all.

And to Glenn Beck, I forgive you.

CONTENTS

INTRODUCTION

Life begins when you live outside your comfort zone.

You may know me from the world of politics, sound bites, and hot takes, but you don't really know me. Yes, you know who I voted for, who I work for, and where I stand on the issues. But you don't know my values, why I am the way that I am, where I come from, and the Tomi behind the "Final Thoughts." I want you to know who I am because I'm probably a lot like you. There is so much that makes me me, and they're probably many of the same things that make you you. I don't want to be your idol, but I would like to be your inspiration, if you'll let me, because I feel that I have stories that are a probably a lot like yours and that maybe you can learn from my mistakes and my grit. Most of us will experience that defining moment (or two or three), where you truly don't know what's next, but you have to move forward regardless. After all, very few people go from perfect job to perfect job or perfect relationship to perfect relationship. I've been there, done that, and learned a lot by coming out the other side, stronger than ever. And that is the point of this book.

I want to share all of that and many of the things that I've gone through in the hopes that they can help you, too. Why am I so certain that my life applies to yours? Because I'm just an average girl from South Dakota from a blue-collar family. I wasn't homecoming queen, a cheerleader, or an athlete. Not even close! I wasn't part of the popular crowd. However, I was lucky enough to be raised by two of the hardest-working people I know. My parents never complained and showed me how to work hard, aim high, and never take shit from anyone. The way they raised me gave me the courage to be fearless, and if not for their example I wouldn't have the strength to stand up for myself. I was taught to question everything and never think that something was true just because someone said it was. I didn't get where I am in my twenties by sitting back and shutting up. I've been fired, sued, dropped, disinvited, heckled, laughed at, slandered, betrayed, and dumped. But that didn't break me. I make it work no matter what life throws at me. I smash those curveballs. And I want to help you do the same. I want you to feel empowered so that you can do whatever you set your mind to.

I don't fit in any mold. I don't look like the rest of the people on TV. I have long, blond hair, two tattoos, and a nose ring and I'm on Fox News. I have a boyfriend and, on the weekends, we go out and drink with my friends. I love God, rap music, and reality TV. (My favorite show in high school was *The Girls Next Door*, about three *Playboy* playmates who were all dating Hugh Hefner and walking around his mansion half-naked.) In other words, I'm not your average conservative chick. I don't read the playbook, I call the plays, and I don't care what people label me because I can't be put in a box. I don't play for safety; I play for honesty, and I'm fearless.

My mom tells people I was born "this way," but I beg to differ. Of course, I would not be where I am today, personally and professionally, if it weren't for my parents, all they have done and the sacrifices they made for me. My parents loved and believed in me. They are the reason why I won't settle for mediocre. They drove the crappiest cars for decades. They skipped vacations and never renovated their house. Sometimes they worked two jobs and yet they never complained. They didn't baby me and, no matter how young I was, they didn't protect me from tough stuff—like alcoholism in our family and money problems. They didn't tell me I was above anyone or that

I was the best; they motivated and inspired me to work hard to *become* my best. My family didn't have a lot of money, so when I went to the University of Nevada, Las Vegas, or UNLV, many of my mom's friends and family questioned why she'd let me go to an out-of-state school when I could go to a local college where the tuition was a lot less. She took so much crap for that, but she had faith in me. She knew how much I'd get out of it and she was right. I promised my parents when I was a little girl that someday I would pay them back for all they've done for me. At age twenty-six, I am blessed to start fulfilling that promise. They are so proud and humble that they still try to pay for our family dinners. I literally have to wrestle the bill out of my mom's hand. Truth is, I could pay for every dinner, vacation, or luxury item for the rest of their lives and still fall short. I am where I am because they stood back and let me spread my wings and open my big mouth.

Of course, my parents have had to deal with that big mouth and my strong opinions since the moment I started talking. When I was growing up, my mom and dad both worked full-time, so Saturday was put aside for cleaning the house. That didn't sit well with seven-year-old me, who wanted to go shopping with my mom, not scrub the bathroom. What to do? I wrote memos detailing how I felt and all the reasons why we should go shopping and not clean. I told my mom that life was too short and gave her suggestions for alternate times we could straighten up. Even at that young age, I had discovered Microsoft PowerPoint and would often create full-blown presentations for that extra little push of persuasion. At first, she resisted, but eventually I wore her down. And that was just the start. To this day, if you ask my mom what adjective she would use to describe me, it would be *relentless*. I'll take that as a compliment. I've always loved to entertain people but when I wanted a camcorder to record my own shows, my parents naturally said, "No." After all, its five-hundred-dollar price tag was way out of their budget. But I was determined, so at ten years old I pushed and pushed and pushed the issue. Finally I convinced my parents to let me buy the camcorder on layaway, and I made the monthly payments. I did this by telling everyone in my family that I didn't want gifts for birthdays and holidays, just money. I also did extra chores around the house to help pad that birthday and Christmas money. In time I paid off the entire camcorder, which I used to create cooking shows with my cousin. I would write scripts and host the perfectly timed shows, and we'd hold up handwritten signs so they looked like titles. (And my poor parents had to sit and watch!) My point is that I always had a reason and I always had a case for everything. My dad still tells every guy I date, "Just accept the fact that you won't win an argument with Tomi."

Naturally, not everyone feels that way, and it seems like everybody wants to take a swing at me. I get slammed by the left and the right. But I've been getting slammed for my political views since the first time I was forthright in expressing them. It was my junior year in high school and, though I was too young to vote, I felt very invested in the upcoming 2008 election. I went to the local Republican county office and asked if they had McCain bumper stickers.

"They're five dollars," they told me. That seemed like a lot of money for a sticker, especially since I thought they'd be free. Still, I bought one and proudly put it on the back of my Chevy Cobalt. One day I was leaving school to go to lunch when an older gentleman pulled up next to me at a stoplight.

"How can you vote for a monster like that?" he screamed out his window.

"Same question back to you, sir," I said before I drove away. (Yes, I used to be a huge John McCain fan. Ya know . . . before full-blown RINO syndrome hit him.) But I wasn't rattled or shaken. I was confident in my candidate and my beliefs. And I still am. I know how to think for myself and be myself. Over the years, people have tried to say that I'm a younger, blonder version of various other women on TV. Wrong. I'm not trying to be the younger, blonder version of anyone. I'm trying to be Tomi. This confidence—politically and in general—is something people ask me about constantly. Wherever I go, the question I get most often isn't about politics. It's this: "You're so sure of yourself, your beliefs and who you are. How?" Girls from fifteen to fifty years old ask me some variation of this every single day! It's because I stand up for myself.

And I don't just stand up for myself for my benefit. I do it because I know there are a lot of young girls watching me and *how* I stand up for myself, which is sometimes more important than just standing up for yourself. Recently I was in Target and noticed a young girl and her mom staring at me. I'll be honest. Because they were Hispanic, I thought they were looking at me because they didn't particularly like me, so I ducked into an aisle to make myself as unnoticeable as possible. That didn't work because the girl, who must have been fifteen years old, approached me. Then she freaked out and screamed, "Oh my God, Mom, it is Tomi!" Her mom came over and told me how much they appreciate that I support law enforcement because they support law enforcement as well. The daughter told me that she was being mentored by a sergeant at the local police department and wanted to be an officer one day. She told me part of the reason she was inspired to join the police force is that people like me stand up for them. That's when it hit me. I don't work in law enforcement but the simple fact that I support them—that I'm young like this girl, and she can relate to me—inspired her to one day take on one of deadliest jobs. That's a huge honor and responsibility. I don't take it lightly.

That's why I mean it when I say that this book isn't about politics. Believe it or not, my politics don't define me. They are part of who I am, but they aren't everything I'm about. This also isn't a book just for conservatives. One of my greatest accomplishments is being able to withstand heat from both the left and the right. This book isn't about trying to make you like me or me defending myself. I want you to get to know me for who I am: the good, the bad, the ugly, and the inspirational. At the end of this book, you might still hate my politics and maybe even hate me, but at least you'll have a better understanding of how I got here. I don't want you to stand up for me; I want you to stand up for you, and I can teach you how to do that.

When I got fired from *The Blaze* and had to deal with a lawsuit, I had been at the highest point in my career and got knocked down to my lowest. But I held my ground, and I'm still here, better and stronger than ever. I wouldn't take back a moment of even my worst experiences, because they taught me how resilient I am. And how fearless. They also made me grateful for every blessing that I have and keep me laser focused on getting where I want to go. I go forth and conquer. I don't let anybody stop my journey and neither should you. I've survived social isolation, terrible boyfriends, awful workplaces, getting fired in front of a million haters, and a lawsuit that nearly bankrupted me. Along the way, I've been coached to be quiet, but lie down and play dead isn't my style.

I always say: once you live without fear, it doesn't get much better. Do no harm, but take no shit! Recently I got a letter from a young girl who wrote, "You are truly an inspiration and voice to every single person who may not have enough heart, guts or courage to stand up for what they believe in deep down. Keep on keeping on." That's what I plan to do and want to help you do, too.

Never Play Dead

Chapter 1

STANDING YOUR GROUND WILL NEVER FAIL YOU.

Lie down and play dead isn't my style.

I've never been too intimidated to say my piece. That's just how I was raised. I can't please everyone, but I will always be authentic, articulate, and unafraid of the backlash. Why? Because if you know what you're talking about and what you believe in and you're willing to fight for that, it will never fail you. I live in California and women come up to me and say, "I can't talk to my friends about being conservative" or "I voted for Donald Trump, and I can't tell anybody." One day while I was working on this book at a coffee shop, a mother came up to me with her preteen daughter and was practically whispering when she told me, "The conservative moms at my kids' school have to have our own secret group." Sad, but I hear that all the time. It's unfortunate that our country is this way, but it will only change if people feel empowered to stand up for themselves.

Standing your ground is not always easy. However, when you do it over and over, it becomes the way that you are, and that adds to your confidence. It makes you feel better about yourself. It sets you free. But I'm not just talking about politics. This applies to your religious beliefs, issues at work, relationships with friends and family members, romantic relationships, interactions with teachers and professors, and pretty much any area of your life.

One night, I was at a neighborhood bar with my boy-friend. A girl around my age was sitting next to me on a bar stool. When she turned around and recognized me, it was like her heart was going to pop out of her chest.

"Oh my God. I'd never thought I'd meet you," she said.

"It's great to meet you, too," I replied, reaching out my hand.

"I've been going through some difficult stuff over the last month, and you've been my inspiration," she said. Then she shared her story: she worked for a group that advocates early detection for breast cancer and raising awareness for women's health issues. It's a female-dominated industry, but she felt like she couldn't tell her boss or liberal colleagues that she was a conservative.

"I'm around women who are supposed to empower other women, but I can't be myself," she said. A month earlier, her female boss appointed a forty-seven-year-old man from outside the organization to oversee this girl's department. From day one, he treated her like crap. He talked down to her, was rude, and acted like she didn't know anything. At first she was going to deal with this horrible treatment, and she did so for weeks. She didn't think she had a choice.

"But then I thought about you and knew that I needed to say something," she told me. "I was terrified, but I finally had the courage to stand up and tell my boss and board of directors that, at this company for women and by women, they were letting a man come in and treat me like crap." The board of directors took note and after that everything changed.

"I call that my Tomi Lahren moment. I was terrified, but once I did it, I felt free," she said. "It was like a weight lifted off of me." I knew what she was talking about. Once you make a habit of standing up for yourself, it's not so hard anymore. Slowly but surely, it becomes part of your daily life. And that's my goal. All I want is for you to find your voice. Yes, it's uncomfortable at first, but the more you do it, the more confident you get. It's like learning how to ride a bike. Initially it's scary, but you get better and better and better. Pretty soon you're not afraid anymore. In fact, you're flying! It's the same with having an opinion and standing up for yourself. If you do it continually, it becomes who you are. You will never reach your full potential in anything if you are not your authentic self or live in a shell of someone else. You need to make the choice: are you going to go through the motions for fear of rocking the boat *or* are you going to fucking go for it with guns blazing?

WHEN I WAS a sophomore at UNLV, one of my journalism assignments was to write an article and submit it for publication. Most of my classmates covered campus events for the school paper. But I wanted to do something bigger. (Are you surprised?) I decided to write an article on students who strip to pay for college. After all, I was in Vegas! I told people what I was doing and as luck would have it a woman in my class had a friend who did this. Malyssa was a twenty-one-year-old women's studies major and self-proclaimed feminist and like most students needed to pay the bills and tuition. Doing so by taking off her clothes never crossed her mind until a local stripper spoke at one of Malyssa's classes, called

Sex, Dance, and Entertainment, a course that explored the sexual side of dance and satisfied her fine arts general education requirement. Malyssa gave it a try and realized that parading naked in front of strangers helped ease her financial issues. I also found out about a circuit judge in Vegas who had worked as a topless dancer in her twenties and was willing to talk to me about how she paid all of her undergraduate tuition by dancing at Cheetah's strip club. Then I interviewed a women's studies professor whose class I'd taken as a freshman. I thought her perspective would be interesting, which it was. Her take was that stripping was just like any other part-time job in Vegas, made especially appealing because the hours were flexible and the pay was great.

When I finished, I submitted the article, called "Lessons by Day, Lap Dances by Night," to the *Las Vegas Review-Journal*, the largest daily paper in the area. They accepted it to run that Sunday. I was thrilled, but not everyone quoted in the piece felt that way. As a courtesy, I'd emailed the article to everyone I'd interviewed in advance of its publication. Journalism 101 is that you *don't* do this, but I wanted to make sure Malyssa felt okay with her quotes since her name would run with the story. The last person I thought would have an issue with it was the women's studies professor. But she did. When I'd interviewed her weeks earlier, we met at

Starbucks and had a really interesting and friendly conversation. But now she was outraged, and not because of *anything* that the article said, but *where* it was being published. She told me she did not want the article in what she deemed a "right-wing" newspaper. I was terrified. I was worried she would come after me or complain to my professor.

One thing people don't realize is that, although I embrace political confrontation, I avoid personal confrontation at all costs. Even today, if I order food at a restaurant and am brought the wrong dish, or if I have a problem with a friend, I really hesitate when it comes to saying anything. Still, I took a step back and asked myself a few questions: Was everything I said in the article accurate? Yes. Were my intentions good? Yes. Were there negative consequences for anyone quoted in the story? No. I knew that I didn't do anything that was ethically wrong and realized that this professor was just trying to diminish me and have power over me. Sure, she was a professor, and I was just a student, but I stood my ground and allowed the article to be published. And each time you do that you build that muscle. You get a little stronger. No matter what it is, stand your ground one time and see how you feel afterward. I promise you that you're never going to look back and say, "I feel bad that I was myself today" or "I feel bad that I expressed myself today." Once you find it within you and you no longer live in fear, life gets so much better. And you'll start thinking, I don't care what comes at me today. I'm going to hit it, and it's going to be fine.

The problem is that we learn how to be ourselves so late in life. Wouldn't it be nice if you could learn how to do it in your early years, not just when you're twenty or thirty or even forty or fifty years old? If you wait, you don't know how to be yourself, and it contaminates everything, including relationships, friendships, and work. Don't get me wrong, it's never too late to find your voice, but the sooner, the better. When I was at the Young Women's Leadership Summit, a four-day conference for young conservative women ages fifteen to twenty-seven, a recent college graduate and Trump supporter raised her hand. She was an intern at a big company in New York City. At a board meeting where the executives in the room were talking about the next round of hiring, one of them asked the other, "Can you imagine if we hired a Trump supporter?" This young intern said her heart raced. She was looking for a job so she felt like she couldn't say that she *was* a Trump supporter.

"What do I do in that situation?" she asked me. This is something I hear *all* the time from young girls and women who can't tell their friends, relatives, colleagues, room-mates, professor, fill in the blank, who they really are.

But how come we're in an environment where women feel empowered to stand up and say #MeToo about things like harassment, sexual assault, and bullying, but conservatives can't stand up and express who they are? Another thing I hear often is people saying that they're afraid to add "Trump supporter" to their online dating profile because they're worried that other people won't want to date them. But if someone doesn't want to date you because you're a Trump supporter, do you want to date *them*? Probably not. Life is too short to care what people on a free app on your phone think of you!

I understand that this intern wasn't comfortable speaking up, but if all the people like her spoke out and shared their experience, pretty soon you'd have a movement and they couldn't ignore you anymore. What happened with Facebook censoring conservatives is a perfect example.

In 2016, Facebook workers suppressed news stories of interest to conservative readers on the social network's influential "trending" news section, according to a former journalist who worked on the project. And these "news curators" reportedly injected stories into the trending news module even if they weren't popular enough to warrant inclusion—or in some cases weren't trending at all. They used algorithms to inject their own bias—

their *liberal* bias—into the process. Facebook promised to fix this, and to give conservative pages and voices a fair shot. But even a year later, Diamond and Silk—two pro-Trump political commentators with millions of social media followers—were informed by Facebook that their videos were "unsafe to the community." Initially they got away with this political bias and leftist control of the message, but eventually enough conservatives got together and spoke up. Then all of a sudden Mark Zuckerberg had to take a look at the situation, and he was like, *Oh crap there are more of them than I thought.* Zuckerberg likes only 115 people's pages on Facebook and mine is one of them. He pays attention to those who make him money. By speaking up, conservatives were showing Facebook that we make them money and if they piss us off we will leave Facebook. That's when Zuckerberg started getting nervous, which is why he did a phony summit about two years ago with people he deemed "conservative leaders." (Glenn Beck was one of them.) Then there was the Senate hearing last June where Facebook was called to the carpet for what they did. My point is that there is strength in numbers. And this goes for anything. You may be too scared to express your feelings about something. You think you're the only one. But when you do it, others will follow, and you will realize how many people support you. You will see that you are not alone.

Liberals have figured this out and use it to their advantage on a daily basis, but conservatives suck at it. Liberals are unafraid to put their political views out there because they have this indulgent, conceited idea that they always have the moral high ground. They aren't worried about offending people. They protest in the streets, shouting their beliefs, and are comfortable walking into any room and saying how horrible our president is. Of course, we know how it also turns their world upside down when they realize not everyone agrees with them. A perfect example is the way many college campuses dealt with students who were distraught over Donald Trump winning the 2016 election. At least one school had a cry-in with students dressed in all black; another planned a late-night primal scream. Other universities offered all sorts of things to comfort students: think counseling sessions, healing spaces, hot cocoa, therapy dogs, Play-Doh, canceled classes, and postponed exams!

Most liberals aren't scared of losing their jobs because they are liberals.

Celebrity liberals have no problem broadcasting their political views, like Alyssa Milano live tweeting from the Kavanaugh hearings and Lena Dunham protesting outside an immigrant detention facility. They have no fear. But as Trump supporters, we do. We don't speak out and tell the world we support Trump. That's why the polls are so wrong, and everyone thought Hillary was going to win the 2016 election: the average person who voted for Trump is afraid to say it. They call these people "whisper voters": those who don't say they support Trump because they don't want to be ridiculed, but do so when alone in the voting booth. It was enough to make it look like undecideds all chose to vote for Trump at the last moment.

Yes, conservatives show up at rallies, and we show up to vote, but we don't band together in public displays of conservatism the way liberals do. We are in the closet, and we need to come out! Not to say, "I'm a conservative, and you need to be one, too," but to show that we're proud of our political views. We built a movement in 2016 and elected Donald J. Trump as our president, but that's not enough. The movement can't live and die with the Trump presidency or administration. It has to be built to last the test of time and shouldn't be tied to one person or president!

I'M SURE YOU'RE not surprised that even as a kid, I loved having a voice and making an impact, which is why I always took part in student government. In fifth grade, eighth grade, and my senior year of high school, I ran for student council president and won. I wanted to figure out how we could get other students involved, because if you have a sense of belonging—whether it's to your school,

your city, your state, your country, or anything else—
you're proud of it. And when you're proud, you're going
to work harder for yourself *and* others. I saw so many
kids who had difficult home lives. Maybe they didn't have
a lot of money or their parents weren't around, and they
thought that if they could at least feel a connection to the
school, they would feel better about their lives.

In high school, I was also a student rep on the Rapid
City, South Dakota, school board. There were only three
students—one from each of the public high schools. I
went to Central, the biggest in the state, which had a very
sizable Native American population. Then there was
Stevens, which was known as the rich kids' school, and
Douglas, the smallest, which served the air force base
students and the surrounding community. During a public meeting, one of the ladies on the board turned to me
and said, "You know, it would be good if Central had a
Native American representative, not a white girl." *How
dare she!* I interviewed for that position. I *earned* it. In
fact, it was my Native American principal who selected
me. And as he said, for him to pick a Native American
kid just to pick a Native American, well, *that* would be
racist. Sure, this woman was three times my age, but I
was not going to sit there and take her condescending
comment. I had no problem telling her how incredibly
disrespectful she was.

"I worked hard to be here, and I'm a great voice for Central," I said. Some people think being outspoken and opinionated means that you're just a jerk. But I knew I didn't do anything wrong. She can have her opinion without trying to diminish me. I stood my ground. And each time you do that you get a little stronger. Of course, you put a target on your back, but you also set the precedent that no one can mess with you. In every instance in my life that I have stood up and did what was right, *not* what was popular or politically correct, the people who were true and honest have had respect. They appreciate that you're not just going with the flow, because it means you're being authentic.

I'm not saying it's easy. When I decided to sue Glenn Beck, I had plenty of moments where I worried. I worried that I was not going to have a cent to my name, thanks to legal fees, and that nobody would hire me. I worried that I'd lose my Facebook page for good. But I had to put that completely out of my mind. Here's what happened: On the morning of March 20, 2017, I was getting ready to come in and do my show, actually drawing on my left eyebrow when my phone rang. It was Jim, one of *The Blaze*'s content managers. He and I had become friends, and I could tell from his voice that he was upset.

"Tomi, your show has been suspended indefinitely. Don't come near the building," he said.

"What do you mean *suspended*?" I asked.

"Your comments on *The View* offended the community." Jim was referring to an appearance on that TV show a few days earlier where I said I was pro-choice because I believed in limited government. It was getting a lot of buzz, and I heard that other *Blaze* employees were bashing me on the radio all morning, so I knew I was walking into an interesting day at the office. But I never thought they'd pull my show. I had planned to discuss the controversy on that day's installment. It would have cleared up *all* the questions and confusion. Too bad I was never given the chance.

"Are you kidding me?"

"We'll give you an update in a few days," Jim said.

"What about my team?" I asked.

"They'll find other projects," he said. The whole thing was shocking. After *The View* taping, I walked off the set to my agent and executive producer, who were waiting for me offstage. They thought I did an awesome job. I also got emails from several *Blaze* employees saying the same thing. I was on top of the world! I didn't think I did anything wrong. I thought I got it right. That was, until the hammer came down.

The thing is this: I *am* pro-choice. So why couldn't I say that? What people don't understand about me is that when I'm speaking about what I feel, I don't calculate it.

There's no strategy behind it. It's not about what's going to be advantageous to me. I don't play for safety; I play for honesty. My beliefs are my beliefs. I don't say anything to get "likes" or to be contrary to the left. Importantly, *The View* also wasn't the first time that I said I was pro-choice. I had talked about it on my show and in other places, like a *New York Times* profile. Trust me, this wasn't some big announcement. But I guess *The Blaze* wasn't paying attention. I wasn't trying to hurt anybody or be in anybody's face, but I also wasn't going to spit out a talking point and say I'm pro-life, because that's not how I feel. On top of this, some people said I sold out because I was on a liberal show. Sold out? Um, did they watch *The Daily Show* with Trevor Noah? Does it look like I'm someone who appeases people because I'm their guest? I don't think so. Does it look like I've built a career on ass-kissing or toeing the line? No.

So basically *The Blaze*, a place that said they were a platform for "authentic and unfiltered voices," fired me for having a voice. Yes, it's a place for authentic and unfiltered voices, as long as those voices agree with Glenn Beck. I should have known this to be the case at *The Blaze*. You see, two weeks after I arrived, I quickly noticed the almost cultlike environment. One of the producers pulled me aside and told me I needed to understand something called the FOG—friends of Glenn—which made up half the people who worked there. "If you're a FOG, you can pretty much get away with anything. But if you're not, be careful," she cautioned me. Just days after I was suspended from *The Blaze*, they called to tell me not to go on social media or TV and not to talk about what happened.

"Just go dark," they said. Seriously? Glenn was attacking me on Twitter and slandering me on the radio. And he wasn't alone. Many of *The Blaze* personalities were following his lead. It really hurt that this was taking place on Twitter in front of thousands of people. I would have appreciated a phone call or email saying, "Hey, we need to talk about this." But no. *The Blaze* chose to go public in the nastiest of ways.

"They're allowed to talk about *me* on the radio and social media, but I can't say anything? I can't defend myself?" I asked my agents.

"I'm sure you've signed a nondisclosure agreement, so I guess not," my agents said. (At this point I thought they were correct about the NDA, but later I remembered this wasn't true.)

"Can I just get out of my contract?" I asked. "I just want to move on."

"No, but they'll have to pay you through the end of it, which is six months."

Are you freaking kidding me? My heart sank to my

stomach. This was surreal. They didn't have to pay me: just let me out of my contract and I'd walk away. I didn't want revenge. I didn't want to slander them. I didn't want to sue them. I didn't want money. I just wanted to *leave.* I was saying, "Let's agree to disagree and let me move on."

I told them I wouldn't even do TV. All I wanted was the freedom to do my "Final Thoughts" segment on my Facebook page. Can you believe they said no? Not being able to comment on issues that mattered at the time, like Syria, and not being allowed to have my voice out there was maddening. What's funny is that *The Blaze* never cared about my page until it started getting views. I filmed the early segments of my "Final Thoughts" from the hallway with little help from anyone at the network! But even though it was my name, *The Blaze* felt they owned it. My Facebook fans had become my family in a lot of ways. When that was taken away, it felt like a huge part of me was shut down.

If *The Blaze* didn't want me, why not sever ties? If I was such a "disgrace" to their network and offended their community so deeply, why not let me go? I'm guessing they figured if I went dark for six months, at a time when my candidate won, it would ruin me and I'd never get another network job.

They made a big deal about this pro-choice thing to

turn the conservatives against me and they silenced me so I couldn't defend or explain myself. They didn't realize who they were dealing with.

A network didn't make me and a network certainly wasn't going to break me.

"FROM NOW ON, you can communicate with my lawyer," I said to *The Blaze* after my agents advised me to hire an attorney. They were practically choking on their words, unsure what to say. After all, who was going to take on Glenn Beck? He *owned* the network. Who was going to say anything? Well, *I* was. Did they think I was so dumb that I was going to let them fire me and sit and get paid to do nothing? Sorry, that wasn't going to happen. After watching my career so far and all the people I'd taken on from the left *and* the right, did they think they were going to tell me to go away for six months and that I was going to take it? *Don't hold your breath.*

I knew my rights and being paid to do nothing is not my style.

I thought getting lawyers involved would solve things so I could move on, but that wasn't the case. It was hell, the darkest time of my life. *The Blaze* could have ruined my career. They could also have bankrupted me by running up my legal fees. Their lawyers stretched things out as long as they could by not returning our calls and making excuses about why they couldn't reach their client. They also wouldn't negotiate. But little did they know, God was in my corner and sent me a gift in Brian Lauten, my savior, a Texas-based lawyer who worked on my case for free. Yes, for free. If he hadn't, my legal bills for him alone could have been $300,000–$400,000. Initially I had California-based lawyers, whom I paid about $100,000, but to go to litigation in Texas, I had to have an attorney who was licensed in that state. (That's an example of God testing you and then sending relief!) Also, without the ability to work, I felt lost.

In April, we went to court trying to get temporary relief, basically saying that while our lawyers decided about my contract, I could go out and get a job. But when the *Blaze* lawyer came to court, he was alone. Neither Glenn nor a single member of the network's management showed up with him. I guess I was worthwhile enough to slander, sue, and destroy but not worthy of their presence in court. I guess the judge wasn't, either. The *Blaze* lawyer said they still wanted my Facebook page. The judge decided that we needed another court date. By now *The Blaze* realized I hadn't signed an NDA, because they couldn't find one, so they requested a non-disparagement order. Funny, because *they* were the ones doing the bad-mouthing and mean tweeting. Well, not even forty-eight hours later an article came out full of lies and slanderous stuff about me. Someone at *The Blaze* leaked this information, which violated the non-disparagement order that *The Blaze* wanted in the first place. They were trying to publicly smear me so I couldn't get another job. Bad move. Really bad move.

We returned to court, where the judge granted my lawyers access to the email accounts of four people at *The Blaze*. This meant that their lawyers had to turn over all electronic documents with any mention of the article. When they did, the evidence was right there in black and white: the emails showed that *Blaze* employees had arranged to have people leak negative things about me to a conservative news source. Since at least a couple of these people weren't in Dallas and had never even met me, *The Blaze* must have thought there was no way the leak could be traced back to them. Wrong. Wrong. Wrong.

Shortly after this discovery, we got a call that *The Blaze* wanted to settle. Interesting timing. That upcoming Tuesday, Glenn Beck was going to have to be deposed on camera by my lawyers. Oh, but it gets better. They were also going to have to fly in the people from around the country who had done the dirty work and have them explain to my lawyers how they leaked stuff about me even though they had never met me. *The Blaze* obviously didn't want that to happen. So, we settled. I got out of my contract, and *The Blaze* had to transfer all ownership of my Facebook page to me as long as I deleted their content. But the story does not end there. We signed the settlement on May 1, but they didn't give me back my Facebook page right away. We gave them two deadlines and almost had to go back to court. Again, they wanted to run up my legal fees and keep me from reaching my viewers and potential employers. Finally, in early August, in the middle of the night, they transferred it over.

Through this whole experience, I had to have faith that I was doing the right thing. Yes, I could have just sat back, collected my salary, and waited it out. But hell no! I was standing up for myself even if it broke me. *The Blaze* was testing my strength, testing how far I was going to go and how much they could mess with me. They didn't think I was going to get attorneys. They thought I was just going to sit back and take it. They thought, Oh, she's twenty-four with no money, and we're a network. We've got her where we want her.

Well, they thought wrong. I was cast aside because I didn't fit the mold. But my message to you is this: It's okay not to toe the party line! You can be an independent thinker, you can take it issue by issue, and that's okay. You shouldn't be told, "You can't sit with us." I never imagined that being honest and staying true to myself would cause so much chaos. I lost fans. I lost friends. I lost my job. But I gained so much more. It wasn't easy, but I wouldn't change a single thing. I learned what's worth fighting for. I learned who sticks around when the going gets tough and who dips out. You may never agree with anything I say or do, and you can call me a lot of things, but weak isn't one of them. Today I feel stronger than ever and am living my dreams. I hold my ground. And I hope you do to. Never give up. Never back down.

When you've been dropped on your ass, don't sit in the corner and feel sorry for yourself. Square your shoulders and tell yourself that no one will get the better of you. You can be fragile like a flower or fragile like a bomb. The choice is yours! It reminds me of a quote I once saw somewhere and love: fate whispers to the warrior, "You cannot withstand the storm," and the warrior whispers back, "I am the storm." Amen!

Chapter 2

I DON'T WANT PEOPLE TO THINK LIKE *ME*. I JUST WANT PEOPLE TO *THINK*.

I have moderate, conservative, and libertarian views. I'm human. I will never apologize to anyone for being an independent thinker.

My boyfriend's best friend since childhood, Jordan, won a recent season of *The Bachelorette*. So he's now engaged to the bachelorette JoJo. They moved to our neighborhood from Dallas, which seemed great because I could finally get to know Brandon's closest friend. For over a month, we kept trying to set up a couples' dinner, but every time we had a plan, Jordan and JoJo flaked out at the last minute. When they canceled plans yet *again* over Memorial Day weekend, I started to realize that this flaking situation was intentional. First, we were supposed to meet them at a bar, but they all of a sudden said they were going home. The next day they told us they were going to the beach, but when we were on our way, they left. "But we're having a barbecue," Jordan told Brandon. "You guys can come to that." And that's when I saw exactly what was going on: JoJo didn't want to be seen in public with me. She was afraid that I'm too controversial. It doesn't matter that I'm her fiancé's best friend's girlfriend. I started to feel this a few weeks back, but I wasn't sure. Maybe I was being overly sensitive, I thought. But now it seemed clear: I could come over to their house because no one would see it. I didn't want to bring it up with Brandon, but I also wasn't going to put myself in that situation. So I told him to go to the barbecue without me and that I had plans with my friends.

"We can meet up later," I said.

Later that night, Brandon met me at a bar. By the time he arrived, I'd been analyzing the situation with my friends for hours.

"Brandon, I'm going to be honest with you," I said. "I know exactly what's going on. JoJo doesn't want to be seen with me in public." At first he didn't say anything, but then he nodded his head.

"You're right," he said. Immediately I started tearing up, so I booked it to the bathroom. Sometimes life sucks. Sometimes I get my feelings hurt and personal stuff gets me. And this got me. So if I'm feeling something, I *will* cry in the bathroom. After a rough week of people trying to trip me at bars and other incidents, it was too much to imagine that Brandon's best friend's fiancée would not want to be seen with me just because she wanted to please *other* people. It was crushing. The thing is, it's not just that someone who is supposed to be my boyfriend's friend does not want to be seen with me. It's that they are actually more on the conservative political side. They may have even voted for Trump, but they will not be seen with me because JoJo is afraid it will ruin her public image, her Instagram endorsements, and her upcoming clothing line. I couldn't meet them at a bar or restaurant, but I could come to their house because I was hidden?

Look, I get that not everyone can stand up for what they believe in and I don't fault JoJo for that. I get that she's launching a clothing line and that she has an image she wants to maintain. I don't hold it against her. But I am hurt. She could have told me directly, and sooner. Having someone tell you, "We can't be seen with you," made me understand even more so why I do what I do: I want to inspire girls to grow up and think, I'm going to stand up for what I believe in. Period. And I'm not going to hang

out with someone or *not* hang out with someone based on
what they are going to do for my popularity/career/fill-in-
the-blank. I'm going to hang out with somebody because
of who they are as a person. I'm going to give them a
chance and remain strong enough to stand up for myself.

However, I am frustrated with anyone who thinks that
being at the beach together means she has to have the
same controversial opinions as me.

News flash: Contrary to popular belief, you can listen
to and respect someone's point of view without absorb-
ing it. And you can agree with parts of what someone
says without agreeing with all of it. Recently I was out
with my boyfriend, his brother, and his sister at a restaurant in the South Bay, Los Angeles. It's not a place we
typically go, because I've had issues with people saying
negative things to me, but we wanted to grab dinner and
they were having Taco Tuesday. When we walked in, a
few people made nasty comments, but I ignored them.
By now I'm used to it. Then, when we sat down at our
booth, I noticed a black woman at a table across the way.
She was looking at me. Next thing I know, she got up
and started walking over to our booth. *What's about to
happen?* I wondered.

"What are you drinking?" she asked. I glanced at my
full glass of water and felt my body tense up. Just a few
weeks earlier, I had water thrown at me at a restaurant

in Minnesota and got cursed out in front of my parents. (More on this in a minute.) *Is this going to be another drink-throwing incident?* I wondered. I really didn't want a confrontation—especially in front of my boyfriend's family. Before I could answer her, she continued talking.

"My name is Kim and I disagree with absolutely all of your opinions, but I'm so impressed with the fact that you stand up for yourself as a woman," she said, and then paused for a few seconds. "I was married to a former heavyweight boxing champion and I never stood up for myself."

"Thank you," I said. Then she pointed to the two girls over at her table.

"Those are my teenage daughters and I really want them to look at you and learn to stand up for themselves, too."

I was pretty shocked. Black women are not my normal demographic. In fact, let's be honest, they are usually life-long Democrats, so they hate me. But I looked over at her daughters and it all clicked. *This* is why I do what I do. Kim's words meant everything to me. In fact, they meant even more to me than any praise I've ever received from conservatives or like-minded people. They validated that I'm doing the right thing. Because the truth is this: I don't want people to think like me. I just want people to *think*. I say that all the time and get a lot of pushback. But it's true. I want people to be bold enough to be themselves, to speak their minds, and to be honest. I don't want to create a bunch of Tomis. I want to inspire girls like Kim's daughters, who are not going to take shit from anybody. Period. It's not that I want her daughters to be conservative. Or I want them to like Trump. I couldn't care less about that.

The biggest criticism I have of other people in the conservative movement is that they want you to walk away from the Democratic Party and the liberals and think like them instead. That's not my goal. I just want you to stand up, speak out, find your voice, and use it. Take it from someone who is labeled "too controversial" on a daily basis. When you live, stand, and speak without fear, everything changes. If that's "controversial," so be it. I don't care. I'm going to stand up for the average American, ranchers, farmers, veterans, the military, our flag, and, yes, our national anthem.

Why? Because a lot of times people think that just because they have a right to do something, it *is* therefore right. For example, let's take NFL players not standing during the national anthem. I believe in Colin Kaepernick's right to kneel and peacefully protest. But the left thinks that just because he has the right to do it, we don't have to the right to comment on it, and that his right to free speech shields him from anybody else having free expression and challenging him. Wrong. I have the *right* to criticize him kneeling. You can say all day long that Kaepernick has the right to do it and people have fought and died for his right. Yes. They have! So I would never say he can't kneel. But what I will tell you is *why* he's picked the wrong battle. The terrorist attack of September 11, 2001, was a horrible tragedy but what stands out even more to me was the day after, 9/12, because the whole country came together under the flag and the national anthem. So, in my opinion, when people tear those things down, you are tearing down all the bonds that we formed after the greatest tragedy in recent memory. You are not trying to better this country. You are trying to belittle and demean what it stands for and the people who have fought for it. So I'm going to ruffle feathers and ignite debate. I'm going to speak my mind and I'm going to inspire you to do the same. But I'm not going to tell you how to think. I don't even want you to think like me. I just want you to think for yourself.

I would never tell a kneeling football player that he can't do it. But I hope I can show a lot of people—including some of them—why they're wrong.

JoJo AND Jordan constantly canceling plans came around the time I was asked to leave a restaurant in Minnesota the day after one of my ticketed shows there. I had flown

my parents in that weekend and on Sunday before our
flights out, we were eating brunch at one of these trendy
rooftop bar restaurants. There had been several hostile
incidents throughout the weekend of people flipping me
off, screaming at me, and taking pictures. Even early in
the meal a girl tapped me on the shoulder and asked me if
I was Tomi Lahren.

"Yes," I said. "Nice to meet you."

"Fuck you," she said. It was like we were surrounded
by sharks. With this in mind, my dad made a plan for us
to exit the restaurant when we were done.

"I'll walk out first, you walk in the middle, and then
Mom will go behind you," he said. As we were leaving,
something hit the back of my head and then I felt water
spill down my shoulders. Startled, I turned around, and
when I did, I saw my mom rushing over to a table full of
people who had clearly thrown the water saying, "What
are you doing?" *No, no, no*, I thought. I raced over to get
my mom and leave when one of the girls started screaming at me.

"Fuck you," she said, her face so close to mine, I could
feel the spit as she spoke.

"You don't even know me," I said. As she continued
cursing and shouting, I noticed a cell phone propped
up in perfect position to capture the whole thing. They
had planned this. I grabbed my mom by the arm, turned

around, and left. Though I knew they videoed the whole thing and might post it on social media, I wasn't going to say a word about it. Unlike other conservatives who relish moments where they can turn the spotlight on themselves and tell the world they were harassed, I'm not a professional victim. The most interesting thing about me is *not* that I had water thrown on me. As I suspected, the people who threw water at me did post the video and soon it went viral. I had to comment.

After this, other incidents quickly followed. White House press secretary Sarah Huckabee Sanders got kicked out of the Red Hen restaurant in Lexington, Virginia, by the owner. Why? Because Sanders works for President Trump. The owner was quoted as saying, "This feels like the moment in our democracy when people have to make uncomfortable actions and decisions to uphold their morals." How does kicking someone out of a restaurant because of how they think have anything to do with morals? Then Kirstjen Nielsen, former secretary of homeland security, was heckled at a Mexican restaurant while she was eating. Protesters marched into the restaurant chanting angrily about the separation of children from their families at the border. They didn't try to sit down and argue with her. They didn't hand her a pamphlet with their take and beg her to read it. They had a powerful person right in front of them, and didn't try to convince her at all.

She may have agreed with them already on some parts of the issue! I would never ask someone to leave *anywhere* because of the way they think. Let's be honest. If you're chasing someone away or you don't want to be around someone who doesn't think like you, you clearly don't have strength in your opinions and viewpoint.

PEOPLE SAY THAT when I go to college campuses or I'm on Fox that I'm trying to make others think the way I do. They say, "All you *do* is tell people how to think." No. Not true. If you really listen to my "Final Thoughts" or anything else I've said, I tell people how *I* think.

I give *my* opinions. Boldly and directly, I put out exactly how *I* feel, but I *never* tell people they have to think the same way or that they're not allowed to have an opinion. I deliver my commentaries and I'm very honest and transparent that what I'm sharing is *my* point of view. I try to speak common sense to start a conversation but I never say, "Think like me."

My goal is to create a jumping-off point for conversation. The biggest frustration I had growing up watching liberal mainstream media like NBC, CBS, and ABC is that they tried to appear neutral when they were not. I would have more respect for Anderson Cooper if he didn't try to play like he's in the middle. The same with

Chris Cuomo, George Stephanopoulos, Robin Roberts, and others. One of the reasons I got into this business is that I have an opinion. There's nothing wrong with having one if you don't try to pass it off as news, because that is subtle brainwashing. When we're talking about college campuses, I don't have a problem with a professor saying, "Guys, I'm a flaming liberal," but when they say, "I'm just being neutral," and then go into all their liberal propaganda, that's what frustrates me.

Be who you are. I never tell people I'm a news reporter, a journalist, or an anchor and that I'm just giving you the news of the day. No. I'm a commentator. Feel free to disagree but at least you see me, the real me, and I'm being honest. I'm explaining my thought process and why I'm passionate about something but I'm not trying to disguise it as news; I'm not trying to trick anybody. To me, the most authentic thing you can do is to be 100 percent yourself so people know where you stand. The problem? Most people pretend they are something else; they try to see which way the wind is going to blow. Yes, sometimes you change your mind about things and that's okay, if you're honest about your journey and your thought processes and you don't do it for fame, money, or votes. If you're authentic, then you don't have to explain yourself.

The problem people face is they feel like they have to explain themselves because they realize they're being found out and things are not adding up. I don't need to worry about things not adding up because I put it in front of your face. I feed it to you on a platter. You don't need to wonder what Tomi's motivation is behind this. You *know* what it is because I'm telling you what it is. I say these are *my* final thoughts. I don't tell anyone these are *the* final thoughts. Often I end by saying, "Those are my final thoughts. Feel free to disagree." Could I be any clearer?

I'm just sharing my thoughts and maybe others will see an issue differently or have a reaction. In college, my goal was not to change my professors' minds; it was to start a conversation so everybody else in the class would think about an issue a little bit differently. Why? Because if someone goes unchallenged, then everyone just follows along and you end up with a bunch of little clones who think the same. And yes, a bunch of conservative clones running around is *just as bad* as a bunch of liberal ones. That's why I have such an issue with some of the new forces in conservative media. Instead of saying, "You're no one's bitch and no one's victim," they try to convince women and minorities that they are victims of the left. Here's the deal: You're only a victim if you allow yourself to be a victim. Yes, you may have been victimized at some point in your life but *victimize* is a verb. You can't change the verb, but you can change the noun—*victim*.

The worst thing we can do to our movement is make

it a conservative version of what the left has been doing for generations. Don't be a conservative because someone told you the left is oppressive. Don't be a conservative because your friends are. Don't be a conservative because Kanye West put on a MAGA hat and went on a rant about it being his superhero cape when he hosted *Saturday Night Live*. Truth is, if we hold up Kanye or even Donald Trump as a savior or idol of the conservative movement, how are we any better than the left with their idolization of Colin Kaepernick or Barack Obama? We aren't. And guess what happens when it becomes about idols instead of the values? The movement dies when Kanye goes back to his leftist roots or Donald Trump leaves office. We can't pin this resurgence of conservatism to a person. It has to be about ideas and values. After Kanye's *SNL* appearance, one of the "fresh faces" in the conservative movement stated he is "one of the bravest men in America" and a "hero." *Wait, what? Are you freakin' kidding me?* You can't criticize the left for holding Kaepernick up as a hero and then turn around and do the same thing with Kanye West. Attention, hypocrite alert! The second we start making our message about race, celebrities, and publicity stunts, we *fail*.

When I post on social media, write articles, or appear on TV, I'm not trying to persuade everyone to be like me. In fact, I encourage you not to. I encourage you to be *you* and that's what I hope you get from watching and listening to me. To be bold enough to be authentically and genuinely *you*. To question everything. To find your own way. Your own path. Your own beliefs rooted in your moral fiber, your religion, your worldview, or whatever it may be. I find it frustrating when people say, "You're so outspoken and you hurt people's feelings. It must mean you're a shitty person." No. it doesn't mean I'm a shitty person. It means I have an opinion that might be different from yours and I'm not afraid to say it. Why does that make me bad? And the truth is this: whether you love what I'm saying or hate what I'm saying, you're having a reaction to it and that's exactly what needs to happen in this country.

I believe we all want what's best for America; we just have different ways of going about it and that's fine. Today's political climate has driven us so far apart that we have forgotten how to agree to disagree. We've also been conditioned that you can't talk about religion and politics—especially conservatives. But the fear of discussing these topics has led to an inability to navigate difficult conversations about difficult topics. That needs to change because political correctness is intellectual dishonesty. There's nothing more frustrating than when people say we need to have a conversation about race in this country, *but* what they really mean is that it's a one-way conversation that only black people can have and that I'm not allowed to talk about these issues because I'm white. But race isn't the only off-limits topic in the world of political correctness.

It's also frustrating when people tell me over and over again that I can't talk about or respond to any of the kids who survived the Parkland, Florida, school shooting in February 2018. *Of course* I'm not attacking them for what they went through. Not at all. I'm sorry they had to experience such a tragedy and I'm not trying to dilute that or take it away from them. However, I wanted to respond when they were talking about gun rights and the Second Amendment, which I did during a "Final Thoughts" after the March for Our Lives. I started by saying that I was glad that young people in this country were exercising their First Amendment rights, rights that generations of Americans have fought and died to protect. These young people, including the Parkland survivors, have a voice and I truly believe that they deserve to be heard. However, they claimed that they "marched for their lives." Understood. But lives are also protected, defended, and saved by good, law-abiding Americans—with guns! Good guys with guns like Stephen Willeford, who helped end the carnage in a Texas church when a man opened fire and killed twenty-six people in November 2017. Lives are also protected by the proper use of guns by trained police

or security officers. The resources officer at Great Mills
High School in Maryland stopped a school tragedy with
his bravery, training, *and his firearm* just a week before
the March for Our Lives. Did the marchers mention either
of them on the signs at their march? No, they didn't.

Their message was more anti-gun and anti–National
Rifle Association than anything else. This demoniza-
tion of the NRA does nothing to solve the problem. The
NRA is made up of nearly five million fellow Americans, people who want what's best for this country, too.
The students and many other people may think the solution is gun control. And we can debate that. *But* they
can't blame law-abiding gun owners and NRA members
for crimes they didn't commit. You don't get to self-
righteously demonize those who disagree with your gun
control agenda. We *all* want to stop school shootings
and gun violence. But if you think the solution is simply
more gun control, you're missing the mark, and ignoring
the facts. If gun laws stopped crime and death, the city
of Chicago—which once had the toughest gun laws in
the country—would have been among the safest cities in
America. But it wasn't, and isn't. Why? Because gang-
bangers, lunatics, and terrorists don't care about gun
laws. We don't love our guns more than our kids or our
fellow citizens. We don't worship our guns, either. We
simply believe in our constitutional right to protect and

defend ourselves and our families. You don't get to chip away at the Second Amendment simply because *you* don't find it useful. I know some people think the U.S. Constitution is dated, old, and irrelevant. But I suggest you crack open your history books. Our Founding Fathers ensured our right to bear arms as a way to protect us from tyranny. And that's as relevant today as it was when the Second Amendment was ratified—as part of the Bill of Rights—in 1791. The first step to oppression is disarming the citizenry. We've seen that pattern again and again throughout history. Our Second Amendment rights mean something, and we will not sit idly by and watch them be arbitrarily corroded. So, yes—march, chant, and protest. But remember, *my* First *and* Second Amendment rights do not end where your feelings begin. The bottom line? No one is going to tell me I can't talk about something because I'm not fill-in-the-blank enough.

We *need* to have those conversations without worrying that we are going to offend somebody. If we don't, that's when misunderstandings happen, and that's when people are uninformed and uneducated. And how are we going to change anything if we don't step up and speak our minds? The Constitution was written *because* our Founding Fathers didn't agree but they still listened to each other. That's why I go on different shows. If I just sit on Fox News all the time, I'm with people who think the way I do and with an audience that thinks the way I do. I'm not impacting anyone. I'm not having a conversation.

Recently the actress Alyssa Milano was going nuts tweeting about border agents teargassing children. I've been to the border, I've met those people, and I know they're not monsters. She was misinformed, but I was willing to hear her side and to learn something. I emailed her publicist and DM'd her, asking her to come with me to meet the border agents and then I'd go meet the great illegal immigrants she was talking about. I made it clear that I wasn't doing this for show. We didn't need to bring cameras; it could just be the two of us. Why? I wanted to have a conversation with her. I don't need to talk to people who already agree with me. I want to talk to people with different ideas; maybe I'll learn something. Or maybe they will. The point is that people are afraid to have different perspectives and I'm not sure why. I'm confident enough in what I've seen, but I'm also open to hearing and seeing your perspective. One of us may very well be *more* right, and we need to find out which one, or else this country will never make any progress. Not surprisingly, I never heard back from Alyssa or her publicist.

Another reason I don't tell people what or how to think is that I don't want anyone telling *me* how to do that. One thing that made me really mad was when we had a Supreme Court justice nominee whom some people supported only so they could overturn *Roe v. Wade.* The nominee himself understood that's not his duty. Yet many conservatives insisted that's what he should do.

First of all, that's unethical. Second, it's unconstitutional, because we don't legislate morality. We don't nominate people to that position just to carry out our religion. We do it to interpret the Constitution. So if you say you are going to put someone on the Supreme Court to interpret your religion and then place that on the country, that's not what the Court stands for. That's not what conservatism is about. You are trying to distribute your religion to everybody else and do it by dictate. You're not doing it by putting your beliefs out there and then letting others draw their own conclusions. And you're not doing it by being an example and living a life of godliness. You're doing it by telling people they need to think like you do or else it's illegal. That couldn't be more contrary to what I believe conservative thought is. Conservatism is about freedom. Imagine that it's one hundred years down the road. We've elected a devout Muslim to the White House and he appoints someone to the Supreme Court and starts legislating *their* religion. How are these conservatives going to feel? Trust me, they're going to be the first ones to go into panic mode. I'm as conservative and Christian as anybody else, but this country is great because we are a nation about freedom, especially religious freedom. So live your life as an example. You can encourage people to live their life through Christ, but don't you dare go to the government to mandate people think like you religiously.

At the end of the day, you don't want to persuade everyone to be like you. Whether someone agrees or disagrees, that doesn't make you wrong. You're just stating your opinion. You don't necessarily want agreement. That's not the point. You want to show people that you have a voice and have them respect it. Don't attack someone just because they think differently than you. This happens to me all the time. People who have never met me say that I'm this horrible monster because I'm a Trump supporter, conservative, and outspoken. Allow people to get to know you and show them otherwise. You have to be able to separate people from politics. The challenge is being able to stand up for yourself around people who disagree with you and *still* have them like you personally. I know this firsthand because I have met some of the kindest people who are liberals. I think some of their ideas are bat-shit crazy, but they are warm and friendly.

For example, even though I think Chelsea Handler's political opinions are absurd, she was kind to me when I was onstage with her at Politicon, a Los Angeles–based convention that's like the Comic-Con of politics. Chelsea had actually reached out to the organizers of Politicon, asking to have a conversation with me. Of course, I accepted. After all, I grew up watching her show *Chelsea Lately* every night in high school with my mom and read all her books. Chelsea was an icon of mine. Still, I was apprehensive, wondering if this would be like the Trevor Noah show where I was told it would be one thing—fun and games—but got sideswiped. Noah visited my dressing room before the show but then turned around and riled up the audience, saying that they should treat me like their racist uncle coming for Thanksgiving. Chelsea also made an effort to seek me out before the show.

"How are you?" she said when she greeted me backstage and gave me a big, genuine hug. I felt the authenticity of it and this, along with the fact that she took the time to do so, calmed me down completely and put me at ease. When the two of us walked out onstage together, the audience of about 1,500 went crazy, clapping and cheering. The roar of that crowd was one of those unforgettable moments in my life where time slowed down and I realized that I was living my dream, standing onstage with someone I watched and admired in high school. *Don't take this for granted*, I told myself. And I didn't. The audience was pretty evenly stacked with fans for each of us and we talked about all the topics—immigration, health care, Trump, etc. Parts of it got contentious but it was civil. It was definitely a conversation more than it was a debate. I learned that politics doesn't need to be gory. You don't need to throw out red meat for people to like it.

After we did that interview, conservative publications asked me to write articles and say Chelsea did this or that or she was stupid. But I wasn't taking that bait. Sorry. Chelsea was really nice to me. As a result, I will never disparage her as a person. The same with Bill Maher and Joy Behar. When I went on *The View,* they said, "Those stupid witches on *The View.*" Yes, I had political disagreements with the show's hosts, but they were friendly and respectful, so I will never turn around and do the us-versus-them thing. I don't do that to people who have treated me with kindness. On the other hand, there are conservative women who have been incredibly mean to me. I may agree with everything they say politically, but they have been so rude that to this day I will duck into a bathroom if I see them coming. (I actually did that for two years at *The Blaze.* Trust me, it wasn't fun.) Now let's be clear: being nice doesn't mean you agree with everybody and that you hold your tongue. You can still have robust debates and discussions. Most of my friends don't agree with the fact that I'm pro-choice and we debate it, but we do it respectfully. My producer at Fox is incredibly pro-life but we're good friends. People from his church ask him, "How can you hang out with Tomi? She's pro-choice." He says what I'd say: "We disagree on this issue but we're friends. Tomi lives her life in the image of God and respects everybody."

It's also important to be friends with people who aren't like you and *don't* have the same beliefs as you. This may be easier said than done for a lot of people. Countless women and men have told me they don't say what they *really* feel, for fear or being rejected, labeled, shunned, or even physically attacked. This has to change. At the Young Women's Leadership Summit, I met a girl in her twenties. "I can't tell my liberal friends that I like you," she told me. This was definitely *not* the first time I heard this. She was into graphic design and had created this picture of me that said, "Stay triggered, snowflakes." It was really cool.

"You're really talented. You should post that," I told her when she showed it to me. But she shook her head. She was terrified to put this creative design and hard work on social media, because her friends would freak out. Still, I guess something I said motivated her because a few days later she posted it on Instagram. She was right; her friends made really mean comments.

"Hold your head up high and stand up for yourself," I wrote to her. And she did! She circled my comment and wrote, "Tomi Lahren commented back!"

Something similar happened after one speech I did on a college campus. A girl who was a sophomore came up to me.

"I'm your biggest fan, but I can't tell my friends," she said. "They don't even know I'm here."

"Why?" I asked.

"They're all liberals and feminists so I'm afraid they won't like me."

"Are they really your friends if they don't like you for your political views?" I asked her. To be honest, most of my friends have totally different views than I. Most are liberals and I don't give a crap what they believe. I care if they're good people and they care if I'm a good person. So if your friends are not going to like you because of your political beliefs, ideology, or religion, or for being vocal about *anything*, then they're *not* your friends. Find a new group, one that's got your back and your front! And I don't mean find a group that thinks just like you do. Find a group that accepts you for *you*. One of my best friends in California is a women's marcher. She hates Trump. She doesn't agree with most of what I say. *But* if anyone ever says anything negative to me or about me, she's the first one to say, "Don't talk to Tomi that way."

People want to segregate themselves into these little areas where their opinions are validated and their feelings never get hurt because everyone thinks like them. They don't want to be challenged or to challenge anyone. But you can't be afraid to have friends on the other side of the aisle. Who knows, you might help open their eyes and you might learn something. You also may be missing out on some really good people. Yes, your best friend could be on the other side of that aisle!

This brings me to another idea that is super-important to me and to living an authentic life: don't play to the hits. When you engage in a conversation about any topic, you become confident in what *you* think. And when you are crystal clear on what you think, you will be crystal clear on who you are, what you believe, and why. And you will never do anything just to make someone like you. I will *never* do or say anything to make money or appease anyone, whether it's a boss/friend/boyfriend/political party. Back when I was a Marco Rubio supporter, my then-manager would say, "Play to the hits. Follow Trump. That will make you more popular." Sorry. I didn't become a Trump supporter because it was popular. I became a Trump supporter because he was our nominee and I believe in a lot of what he says and I can get behind him. But I came to that conclusion alone, *not* to please anyone. I'm not afraid to go against the conventional wisdom of my political party and how I'm "supposed" to think and believe.

At the end of the day, can I go on Twitter and type a bunch of shit about being pro-life and defending babies to get 10,000 retweets and 15,000 "likes" from conservatives? Yes. I can. But will I do that? No. I will never try to push a political belief because I think it's going to advance my career. You have to have integrity. I'm not afraid of the backlash because I don't think, *If I say this, I'm going to lose followers*, because I don't care. I'm not worried about losing fans because I've disappointed them or because of my opinions. I'm worried about losing *myself* trying to please other people, and I won't ever let that happen.

I will stand up for anyone and anything if it's *right*. It goes back to the Glenn Beck lawsuit. I was willing to stand up for something even when it cost me my job. I will always be honest. I will always have integrity, which means that I am willing to lose everything rather than be fake and cower. In my opinion, it's horrible to live in a shell of yourself where everything you do is calculated. I don't calculate anything. I never look at someone and say, "I'm going to do this because it will help my career" or "I'm not going to do this because it will hurt my career."

I'm confident enough in my skills and talents to know the people who follow me don't follow me for who they *think* I am; they follow me for what I am and who I am. They follow me because they believe that no matter what, they're going to get *me*. They are not getting calculated Tomi who just wants to sell stuff on Instagram or who is just trying to be a cheerleader for Trump. They are going to get Tomi. Period. And they know I will tell the truth. No, the truth isn't fair, but it's the truth and sometimes it hurts. I want girls and women to be able to do that, to stand up to the mean girls at school and in life who pick on them, and to the professors who say they can't be a conservative, and to stand up for themselves when anyone around them says, "You can't do this" or "You can't do that." I want them to stand up for themselves when someone tells them, "You are not enough." Because if you can stand up for yourself, you are *more* than enough!

People *will* like you more when you go along with the crowd and play to the hits. But they don't like you for *you*. They like you because you think like they do. They like you because you're validating them. Forget that! Speak your truth. If they don't like it, tough. And if they turn into haters because you state your truth, that's *their* loss, not yours. Move on. I don't try to win over haters. I'm not a jackass whisperer. And neither are you.

Chapter 3

YOU DON'T HAVE TO BE
A JERK ABOUT IT.

*Free speech isn't just saying what you want to say;
it's hearing what you don't want to hear.*

Awhile back, a former friend of mine who is the founder
of a conservative college campus organization invited me
to give a speech at the University of California, Berkeley.
Normally I get paid a lot of money for these speeches, but
he was a friend and it was Berkeley, so I canceled a paid
appearance and told him I'd do his event for free.

"Just let me know when I can tweet about it," I said. A
week later, I still hadn't heard from him.

"Do you have the graphics?" I emailed him. "We
should start promoting this thing." I was shocked when he

sent them to me. I had equal billing with a girl whom I'll call Jane, someone he had plucked from obscurity. (You may know who I am talking about.)

"What the hell is this?" I asked when I texted him. He stammered his way through an answer, telling me that he thought it would be good for us both to be there.

"But you can't do that without asking me *first*," I said. I could see what was going on: he was trying to use me to promote the event, get all the headlines, and thrust his new star into the spotlight.

Sorry. I wasn't doing that. We argued about it, but he wasn't moved.

"I'm not going to be part of this," I told him. And I wasn't. I wasn't going to allow him to create a bunch of fire and controversy using my name as a ploy to promote someone else.

On another note, I was also disappointed in his lack of loyalty, a trait that is so important to me that I make a list of all the people I can't trust.

Shortly after I said that I wasn't going to do the speech, Jane sent me an email attacking me, essentially saying I wasn't as famous as I thought I was. The gist was this: I don't even know who you are. You're not on my radar, and you're threatened by me. I was stunned. There are plenty of women in this industry who say negative things about me, like Dana Loesch, but I would never send them an email. They've have been in the industry longer and work hard, so I respect them even if I don't particularly like them.

Instead of responding rudely, I sent a nice email telling Jane that it wasn't her fault. I was angry with the way it had been handled by my former friend; I felt blindsided and like I was being used as a prop. I told her that I didn't want there to be any bad feelings and that I hoped she understood. She never responded. I sent another email saying, "I don't feel good about this. Can you give me your phone number so we can talk this out?" I truly felt bad. Although it may have come across as petty, that wasn't the point. I felt like I was being taken advantage of by someone I trusted. Again, she never responded. But the story gets even stranger.

Shortly after this, Kanye West tweeted his support for Trump and, as a result, everyone was jumping on the Kanye bandwagon. They kept saying things like "Kanye's going to save the black community." But I don't believe that *one* person can save a community. You have to save yourself. It's great to inspire and empower people to think and speak for themselves. In my opinion, this had less to do with free thought and Trump and more to do with Kanye promoting Kanye. Our president did not win the election based on the whims of the celebrity elite; he won because he focused on the average American. Also, I

don't think we should make any celebrity a messiah, and
I don't believe in tying yourself to someone who is a loose
cannon, who does things to get attention and who told
TMZ, the celebrity gossip show and website, that he was
on opioids! That's a mistake because then when they do
something crazy, we all look bad and it backfires.

A similar thing happened with Roseanne Barr. When
she made a racist tweet about a senior adviser to Barack
Obama, conservatives did mental gymnastics to try to
justify it, to make it seem okay. Well, guess what? It's not
okay! They thought all conservatives should give her a
rubber stamp and support her because her TV show was
seemingly pro-Trump. Should we pin her to the cross for
her tweet? No. But we can't be the kind of people who
stand up for others who are indefensible. What she said
was wrong and disgusting no matter what side of the aisle
you're on, whether you're political or not. If you're a human being, then what she said was wrong.

We need to stand up against that regardless of party
lines and candidates. You can go after liberals or conservatives as a group, and we can go after ideas and laws
and policies. However, we shouldn't make it about people. If you want to start a real movement, it always has
to be about ideas and not people. We can't forget all of
our morals and values to defend someone because she's
kind of on "our side" or "our team." I don't like that mob

mentality, and I don't like teams. It's the same thing when CNN's Jim Acosta pushed the arm of a White House aide when she tried to take his mic at a Trump press conference. Conservatives went crazy, saying that he assaulted her. Look, I think he's a buffoon, I can't stand his network, and maybe he was rude, but watch the video yourself. He did not assault her! Come on! You can't criticize what the left does and then turn around and do the same thing. This whole idea of a "side" or "team" doesn't work for me. The idea that if my team does it, it's okay. No. My team is the American people. Which brings me back to Kanye. He might like Trump, but I don't agree with someone who says that slavery is a choice. Just because someone supports our political beliefs, what they say is fine? No. It's about right and wrong, which is why I don't care that Kanye supports Trump. Kanye is not the messenger for our movement.

When I discussed Kanye on "Final Thoughts," a lot of people criticized me, which brings me back to Jane. Around the same time, Kanye tweeted about her, saying he likes the way she thinks. Of course, she rode the coat-tails of that publicity and got on her high horse saying that she was going to be the vice president in 2024 (referring to the fact that Kanye said he was going to run for president in the same year). Obviously, this girl took what I said personally, but she didn't reach out to me privately. Instead, as part of her newfound notoriety, she proceeded to "like" nasty social media comments about me. It was very petty, and I was not going to engage publicly. Stooping to that level didn't benefit me, and if she thought she was going to bait me into an uncivil or contentious pissing contest, she was dead wrong. I don't play that game because, quite frankly, I don't need to. Think about it, if I punch downward all I do is bring someone else *up* who doesn't deserve to be there. Why would I do that? If I have a problem with someone personally, I don't do it online—especially because that's what she wanted me to do. I'm not stupid. Friends texted me things like, "Do you want me to go after her on Twitter?" No. I don't. Because all that does is make *her* light shine brighter. It would have made her name bigger and given her publicity. Sorry, that was not happening. Then other people tried to bait me, saying things like "You're in a feud." But it takes two people to be in a feud, and I wouldn't engage.

Look, I don't like Jane and I never will. There's no law that Jane and I have to be friends. What she is working on doesn't consume my daily thoughts. I don't spend time obsessing over people. I often get asked which celebrities I like. On top of my list is Taylor Swift. People have said the nastiest things about her—like she can't sing, she's ugly, and she's annoying. Yet every single time, she rises above it and dominates even harder. She doesn't have to say mean things about her critics. She doesn't need to.

She responds *only* through her art form, and she inspires girls along the way. And you don't need to respond to your critics, either. Don't sink to their level. Don't let other people pull you into the mud!

This doesn't mean that I wasn't upset. I was mad. I was hurt. I'll be honest: I was jealous. I was jealous that Jane was getting so much of the kind of attention I usually get. I thought, *What am I going to do? How am I going to get back in the headlines? In the public eye? How am I going to make sure I'm the number one person in this industry? Maybe I should say something!* Then I took a step back. I thought, *No. That's not you. You're not going to be happy with yourself later.* I realized how ridiculous this was and that I didn't want to be a jerk about it. Everyone gets jealous and feels insecure, but you have to tell yourself, "I don't want this feeling." I had to get over it. I had to remind myself that flowers can bloom next to flowers and that it doesn't take anything away from what I'm doing. Never make it about other people. The only way to succeed is with ideas.

So there are two points I want to make here. First, people are going to try to bait you, to get you angry. They want that part of your personality to come out. But don't respond. Mastering the ability to control your reactions is something I've been working on and something I suggest you work on, too. Take the long view. Have foresight.

Know the career path you want to take and have a laser focus on that. Don't let anybody stop your journey. That's why I've had more than fifteen minutes of fame. The only piece of advice that Glenn Beck gave me that I will carry through life is that I don't want to be a shooting star, I want to be a sun.

The goal isn't to be hot shit at this moment; the goal is to outlast and stay the course. Shooting stars burn out. This shit is a marathon, not a sprint, and I run seven miles every morning for a reason. Grit beats flash. The best revenge is having enough self-worth not to seek it. And truthfully, you don't need to seek revenge because karma is a bitch.

My second point: Yes, I was petty and jealous for a week. I was insecure and upset that Jane was the new thing and I felt like I was falling to the wayside. But then I had the strength of character to get over it. So don't waste your time being jealous of anyone else. Because the moment you start worrying about other people, *that's* the moment when you stop focusing on yourself, and you start sliding. That's when the crown slips! Keep your head down, focus, and keep your eye on your little piece of the pie instead of worrying about what other people are doing.

It's toxic to let yourself be jealous. Yes, there are going to be people who challenge you and who are going to be impressive. You might think they are better than you at something and they actually might be. It's tempting to cut them down to make yourself feel better. But you don't have to run people over to have success. I mean, we've all had those moments when a new girl comes into the room/office/classroom/fill-in-the-blank, and you think, Oh crap, because you're jealous of her. But instead of admitting that she's smart, pretty, or whatever is threatening us, we tear her down. Come on, you've done it. I know I have. We think (or, even worse, tell someone else), "Look at her hair; it's ugly. Look at her clothes; they're not that cute." We try to rip her apart. Forget that. Know what *you* bring to the table and do your own thing.

Also, if you do the right thing and you sit back, karma will take care of people. When someone is a fake and a phony, the world discovers. I didn't need to worry about bringing Jane down because she'd do it herself. The things I knew about her were true, so I didn't have to be the one to expose them. All I had to do was sit back and let her expose them herself. Don't use your energy to go after people, because if they are truly everything you think of them—they are shitty people, they are frauds, fakes—they will show that. People will reveal their true colors. You don't need to do it for them. And then you stay out of the mud. Once the fraud came out, Jane had to lash out and talk about my "failed career" and attack me as a person because her back was against the wall.

Here's one thing to note: usually when people come after you and call you things like racist, vile, or stupid, pretty much they're talking about themselves. Jane was no different from Glenn Beck, where once you point out that the emperor has no clothes, they lash out and try to bring you down.

Give everyone a chance. Don't give them a *million* chances but give them *a* chance. There is someone out there who hates you because of what someone else said about you. But they've never met you. It makes me think, How many times do we discount people because of what other people say about them? You don't know what they can add to your life, and you don't know what they're going through. You don't know anything about them except what someone else told you or what you saw on Instagram. We have to give people a chance, not immediately cast them aside. That could be your best friend someday, and you don't even know it!

A few months after Jane attacked me on social media, she was supposed to give a speech at that year's Young Women's Leadership Summit. She was in a bit of hot water for her comments on the #MeToo movement, and everybody was attacking her. I heard that the audience planned to boo her when she took the stage. So in my speech, which was before hers, I tried my best to tell them not to do this. We are more than whatever we said in the heat of the moment, and we are more than a stepping-stone to something bigger. If you don't like what she said about something, get out there with a better message. Don't just decide you hate her now and drown her out with boos. I don't like the girl, but I will never gang up on her when she's down because that's the easiest thing in the world. That's just weak! The girls who say mean stuff about me when I'm down or like negative tweets about me never have the balls to come after me when I'm on top. (They also don't have the balls to say any of these things to my face.)

When people talk to me about the girls who threw water on me in Minnesota, they say, "You should have hit them." But why would I do that? That's what they *wanted*. You might not have water thrown at you, but you may have girls who are saying mean things to you on Instagram or Facebook. Don't react to it. Don't play into their game. At the end of the day, when I think about those girls who threw the water, I hope that someday they reflect on the incident and are embarrassed by how they acted. Instead of being a mean girl right back at them, I'm going to pray for them because those are the people who need guidance.

We often complain that there are not enough women in high positions in this country. Too many women still have the mind-set that men are only going to let a few of us get to the top. That's not the world we live in anymore. But we see another woman doing well, and we don't support her. We are threatened by it. A lot of people don't like those who excel. So we make fun of her outfit, her hair, her intelligence, and her weight. But it's not worth it. Jealousy is a crappy feeling, and falling victim to it will throw you off *your* game. You do not need to battle these people. You don't need to demonize them because they threaten you. Be honest with yourself. If you admit that you're jealous, you'll get over those feelings so much more quickly. We spend so much time worrying about things that we can't control.

All I can do is control what *I* do best. The truth is, you don't want to be someone else. You want to be the best version of *you*. And you don't have to cut people down to do that. Be yourself. Be the best *you* can be. There are other great women out there, and that's okay. Don't talk badly about them. Instead let them motivate you. Let them inspire you. Give them a smile and a handshake. Call them your sisters. If you ever get a chance to treat them how they treated you, I hope you choose to walk away instead.

PEOPLE EXPECT ME to be angry, abrasive, and bitter, but I'm not. I have a big heart, an open mind, and a strong sense of who I am. I'm brave enough to say what's on my mind and I want you to be, too. But it's *how* you say it that matters. Yes, I know what you're thinking, I am often aggressive, passionate, and sassy in my "Final Thoughts." *But* I know how to adapt to my company. Hear me out.

When I do speeches on college campuses, many students tell me that their professors say things they don't agree with, but they're afraid that speaking up could affect their grades.

My response? "Say it. Stand up for yourself." You can be respectful. But you can also tell them that something doesn't sound quite right to you. Not only is it a free country, but you're paying to be there. You have to lift up your voice and speak your truth because no one else will. I know this firsthand from my experience at UNLV. Even though I was in a journalism program, my professors were all very forthright with their liberalism. Sometimes it was really in your face, but I had no problem questioning them and probing deeper. My senior year, I took a class called Sports and Media. We had a visiting professor who took issue with our athletic teams being called the UNLV "Rebels." He said it was a reference to slavery. But that wasn't true, and I told him so. "Rebels" comes from the fact that UNLV was originally based in Reno, but then broke off to have an extension campus in Las Vegas. It doesn't even make sense, because Nevada is the Battle Born State. It was brought into the Union during the Civil War so its citizens could vote for Lincoln in 1864.

The same professor also had a problem with the school's female dance team being called the Rebel "girls." I would go to bat against him—and other professors—all the time, not to change their minds but to show them the other side. I wanted to start a conversation so everybody in the class would think about an issue a little bit differently. I would *not* sit back and allow my liberal professors to indoctrinate my classmates with their bullshit. If I just sat in the corner and kept my mouth shut, I would have been contributing to the problem. I am sick of hearing conservatives complain about liberalism on college campuses when many do *nothing* to challenge it. Yeah, professors are generally liberal, and yes, they brainwash students, but that's only half the problem. We can't just blame professors. What are *we* doing wrong? Why do young people leave college or other academic institutions as social justice warrior leftists? Well, it's because we have failed to inspire them to stand up for their beliefs and values. They walk in without the confidence to express themselves, and they walk out liberal robots. It's an epidemic, and college campuses are a battlefield, made worse by featuring anti-Trump and pro-Hillary classes as part of their course offerings. We will not win the battle, much less the war, if we don't teach young people to stand their ground. Heck, the liberal students and teachers do! Why don't we?

I've always felt this way, even back when I was in fourth grade. As most students do, we learned about slavery and Native American history. But we were only learning one perspective, even in the conservative state of South Dakota. I knew this because my father is a big history buff whose forte is the Wild West and Native American culture. It's something that he talked about all the time at home, which is why the school version of this history didn't seem right to me. It's not that the atrocities my teacher discussed *didn't* happen; it's that we heard only one side of the story.

The Dakota War of 1862 had two sides. Yes, settlers were encroaching on Dakota land, but the response was the cold-blooded massacre of hundreds of civilians. It's an awful chapter in American history, with desperate people killing each other for meager resources. That one side started it does not excuse either's human rights violations. However, that's not how it was taught.

It was less about the history and more about why I should feel bad for being a white person and how my ancestors were monsters. This didn't sit well with me. But—and this is key—I questioned my teachers respectfully. Are there going to be repercussions if you stand up for yourself? Yeah, if you're rude about it! But if you approach it the right way, anyone who is truly insightful and decent will appreciate the fact that you care enough about what they're saying to have a counterargument. My teachers and professors liked that I had a point of view and that I confronted them in a respectful way. They liked that I was listening. In fact, years later I asked that same UNLV visiting professor to be a guest on my One America News Network show, and he did so gladly. Power respects power. What else can they do but listen? Free speech isn't just saying what you want to say; it's hearing what you don't want to hear. By the way, most educators are painfully self-indulgent, so don't be surprised if they take it as a compliment that you challenged them!

Ask yourself, do you want people to agree with you or do you want them to respect you? They are not the same thing. Your friends, college professors, or parents might never agree with you, but the way you present your opinion will determine whether they respect you or not. If you and I have an argument and you say, "You're a Nazi," then I don't have any respect for you, because you called me a stupid name. Like everyone else, when someone says something, I think, Okay this is what he said, and this is my reaction. Those are my first thoughts. However, I take some of the raw emotion out of that unfiltered opinion, and those are my *final* thoughts. Why? Because you can express how you feel, but you don't have to be a jerk about it.

No matter what you think of my politics, I can promise you that no one has ever walked away from an interview, TV appearance, speech, or dinner table conversation thinking that I was mean or disrespectful. People will never forget the way you treat them. I try to follow my rule that I'm kind to everybody in person and treat them with respect—whether I agree with them or not. For example, if I saw Colin Kaepernick eating breakfast with his family, I would never go up to him. But if for some reason I *was* going to approach him, I'd shake his hand and say, "You and I don't agree on anything, but I respect your platform." I would *not* throw something at him or be rude. I am not one of those people who go around and try to antagonize others. I live in Los Angeles, but I'm not going to go to West Hollywood and wave my Trump support in people's faces to cause a reaction. I would never do something to rile people up on purpose, because that's disrespectful. I don't operate that way. I'm even kind to those I *know* don't like me. Reporters from *TMZ* found me at the beach one weekend. I didn't know what kind of story they were going to do, but chances were it would not be positive. Still, I was courteous and kind when I saw them. And they acted the same way to me because I earned their respect.

Here's another reason why you shouldn't be a jerk: other people see how you act in the world, and it forms their impression of you. Even before my *View* appearance and getting fired from *The Blaze*, Glenn Beck was disparaging me very publicly. A few months after the 2016 elections, I was going to do Bill Maher's show. When I touched down in Los Angeles I saw a Twitter notification. Someone tweeted, "If we want to save this country, we need to start at home with Tomi Lahren." Glenn tweeted back, "I know."

And this was when I *worked* for him! *Before* any controversy.

So I shouldn't have been surprised that *The Blaze* team was churning the waters every day during the lawsuit. They would post mean things about me and write articles citing "anonymous sources" or "someone with knowledge of the situation."

Then, a month after I was fired, and just as I was about to give a speech at East Carolina University, *The Blaze* came out with a countersuit. All their claims were BS and they didn't hold any legal water, but they were still putting negative information about me out in public. They said that I was a diva who would yell at the makeup team, scream at the crew for not turning on my space heater, and showed "a general disdain" for people who worked on my show. This was devastating. My parents are blue-collar through and through! My mom works for a bank and at one point had a second job as a waitress in a bar and my dad works for Target Corporation. How can I treat people poorly who are doing jobs *just* like my parents? Jobs that I truly respect and people I truly care about. Would I want anyone to talk down to my parents? Never. So to think that I would do that to the crew members, saying the F-word and bossing them around, really got me. Even worse? I was *friends* with the crew. Yet they couldn't defend me or say anything because *The Blaze* was buttoned up with nondisclosure agreements and they were too scared to defy crazy Glenn and risk their jobs. Long after the lawsuit was over, after the umpteenth round of layoffs at *The Blaze,* one of the makeup artists texted me and said, "I was always behind you but couldn't show it there. Peace out, mofos! Glad you're successful and speaking for us!" I knew it! I knew the great people remaining at that hellhole had my back and just couldn't stand up for me at the time for fear of getting fired.

The Blaze was going after my character and it hurt. People think I'm tough and that things don't bother me. Well, *this* bothered me. *This* was painful. Honestly, why would someone set out to hurt another person when it doesn't benefit them in any way? They were spreading lies about me and took away my Facebook page because it's where people could connect with me. Without it, I couldn't reach anyone. *The Blaze* knew my value, and they knew that other networks were interested in me, so they planned to nosedive me before I could get another job. They were trying to make me damaged goods. I didn't want money or revenge. I didn't want to hurt anybody. I didn't want to ruin Glenn Beck. I didn't even want my job back. But they still tried to hurt my career. How could anyone be so evil? They chose the path that would hurt my career the most.

Even *after The Blaze* lawsuit was settled, Glenn couldn't help but talk about me. He came out and said, "I should have fired her the day I saw her in the hallway." *Huh?* The first time he saw me in the hallway, he hugged me and welcomed me to *The Blaze*. Still, I didn't go out and bad-mouth Glenn—even when I realized that I didn't have a nondisclosure agreement and could say whatever I wanted. I never tweeted a disparaging thing about him or anyone at *The Blaze*. Why? Because while most people see things just a few inches in front of their face, I see things two miles in the distance. I saw the big picture and knew that future employers were watching me. They could see that, regardless of what Glenn or anyone else said about me, I didn't slander them. They could see me take these hard knocks and weather them.

That said, it wasn't always easy to keep my mouth shut and take the high road. I had Harvey Levin from *TMZ* calling me during my seven-mile morning runs.

"Hey, the Beck team is talking, and they're telling me a ton of stuff about what's going on with you," he'd say.

"Sorry, Harvey. I'm not going to talk about this."

"It will just be on background," he urged me. "We can say it was a friend of yours who told us."

"My lips are sealed," I replied. Of course, it would have been *so* easy for me to say, "Yeah Harvey, let me tell you some shit about Glenn and the people who work there. Let me pull back the curtain." But I never played dirty. I knew that it was more important for me *not* to do it. I knew I would get my day. I had to be patient. Even now, as I write this, I'm not trying to bash Glenn. I'm sharing my story to show you that if you stand up for yourself, do the right thing, and pick your battles, eventually *you* will be living your dream and the *naysayers* will be putting their mansions up for sale and looking like clowns.

I also assume that *The Blaze* was hoping I would freak out and give them a reaction. They wanted to drag me into the mud with them. But why would I do something that doesn't help me? You may not have a lawsuit or someone like Glenn Beck going after you, but you will probably have people disparaging you or talking about you, so here's what you've got to remember: people say these things because they want a reaction out of you. Don't give it to them. Don't let them disturb your peace. Just keep going. They *want* you to freak out. They *want* to make you look bad. When people are trying to get a rise out of you, they're trying to get you to fall off your game. And why give them any attention? Glenn and other *Blaze* staffers wanted to make me unemployable. They wanted me to lash out so other networks would look at me and go, "Wow. She's explosive. We can't hire her." Why would I ever give them that?

On a side note, I'll tell you this: If I sit down with Glenn Beck one day, which I'd love to do, I would look him in the eye and say, "I'm mad at you because I believed in what you were doing and you let it fade." It was like the best of times and the worst of times for me. What I'm most angry about is not that he fired me, tried to bankrupt me, or tried to ruin my reputation; I'm angry that he destroyed a network that could have been revolutionary. That said, and as much as I don't like Glenn, I owe him a lot, just like I owe Mr. H from my first network, One America News, a lot. Both of them saw me and gave me a shot. They gave me freedom at work that I may never have again, although my ultimate goal is to get it back. I did not like working for Glenn Beck, but I loved my job there and he took it away just because he was angry and spiteful.

ALL THIS BRINGS me to the topic of mean girls, because Glenn Beck is no different than the mean girls in high school. (I hate to break it to you, but those bitches don't just exist in school; they are everywhere, and they're all ages and sexes.) Recently, I was waiting to get into a bar. When the bouncer recognized me, he let me by-pass the line in front and go through the side entrance. This whole group of girls was behind us and, thinking they were with me, the bouncer let them in, too. But they didn't care about this VIP treatment. They walked past me and glanced my way and one of them said, "Your nails are f-ing ugly. You're a nasty bitch." First of all, my nail polish looked fine. Thank you very much. Second, and much more important, I can't imagine being mean to someone—someone I don't even know—just to be mean. Out of the blue! That same night, a college-aged kid came up to me at the bar and tapped my arm. "I just want you to know that we all hate you," he said. What? Who touches a woman he doesn't know on the arm? Just to be rude? Did his comments make me feel good? No. They did not. But the truth is, I feel sorry for this guy. It took every ounce of his courage to psych himself up to walk over and say something nasty and disgusting. Did that make him feel good? Did he feel validated because he came up to me and told me that everyone hates me? Did he move closer to any of his personal goals in life? I don't think so. I think he probably lives a very bitter life, while I'm very happy with mine and 100 percent myself. I would have respected him if he told me *why* he hated me and what his issues were and said it without being a total jerk.

But he's not the only one. Recently I was getting ready to do my "Final Thoughts" about *Roe v. Wade* when it leaked in the press that I had a small part in a pro-life movie. I played the daughter of a pro-choice Supreme Court justice, but no one took the time to find *that* out. Instead, everyone was saying, "You're pro-choice, but you're in a pro-life movie." I was so frustrated! Even the PR department at Fox called me in a frenzy.

"Are you pro-choice or pro-life? What are you?" they asked. "You're confusing people." Um, yeah, that's because it's a confusing issue! I think there's a middle ground in America between baby killer and Jesus freak that most people exist in, myself included. Abortion in America isn't black-and-white, and neither is my view on it! I'm anti-abortion, but I'm pro-choice. I would never get an abortion, and I would never tell anyone to get an abortion. I've had friends in that position, and I've tried to counsel them against it. Still, I don't feel right having the government tell a woman that she is restricted from having an abortion. I would feel like a hypocrite if I said that. After the first trimester, I do think there is some room for the government to intervene because at that point it is an unborn child that could be viable on its own. But in the first trimester, I don't think we need the almighty government telling these women what to do. I don't think there's a place for that. They don't have to agree with me, but I wish some pro-lifers could see that side.

Regardless of this and the fact that my fellow conservatives and Trump supporters wouldn't like it, I went forward and shared my take on *Roe v. Wade* on "Final Thoughts." Why? Because I am always true to my beliefs despite the party line. In my opinion, pressing for a Supreme Court decision to overturn *Roe v. Wade* would be a huge mistake. Yes, the new high court vacancy was a huge opportunity for conservative values and principles. I got it. And I understood the passion behind the pro-life movement, but still, to me it was a mistake to use conservatives' power and pull to challenge a decision that polls showed most Americans supported. In general, we lose when we start tampering with social issues and overturning this one is unlikely to succeed. Legal tradition makes it harder to overturn a past decision unless there are strong grounds for doing so and a departure from precedent like *Roe v. Wade*, which has since been upheld up by many other cases, is even harder to come by. Fighting for this and alienating Democrats, moderates, and libertarians only to lose in the end was a risk that I didn't think was worth taking. And I was saying this as someone who would personally choose life but also feels like it isn't the government's place to dictate. I ended that "Final Thoughts" by saying that I believe the way to encourage anyone to choose life is to treat her with compassion, understanding, and love—not government regulation. After all, let's be honest: the government does few things well, and I believe regulating social issues is an area where it fails. Let the churches, nonprofits, and community groups step in, not almighty Uncle Sam.

What's interesting is that there are many Republicans who agree with me; they're just not as vocal about it as I am. (Shocking, right?) In fact, you would be surprised by the number of them who came up to me saying, "Good for you, and by the way, I feel the same way about abortion." Of course, no one said they agreed with me after I explained my take on "Final Thoughts." Instead everything escalated. I got raked over the coals by the left *and* the right. People wrote articles, blogs, and tweets saying that I don't understand what it is to be a conservative, that I don't understand the Constitution, and that I'm just dumb. According to these people, the only reason I've gotten where I am professionally is that I'm pretty. Even worse? Former colleagues and friends "liked" these comments.

A politically conservative website posted an op-ed called "Tomi Lahren's Six Lies About SCOTUS & the Right to Life." Another article said that the reason I'm pro-choice is that I had an abortion. That's a lie and a pretty big stretch. Funny how some of these people got their first opportunity to be on television on *my* shows, yet they were like "Let's tear her down" and "We can try to take the crown." I don't hold grudges, but I do make mental notes. I did just that when it came to all the people who jumped on me about the pro-choice thing and "liked" all those nasty tweets, hoping they could sink me. Why? Because when I'm on the rising tide again, they'll be the ones trying to kiss my ass and I'll remember them.

It goes back to typical mean-girl shit from middle school when you have a group of friends and all of a sudden one of them gets cast out, so the other girls pile on. They attack her. They call her names. They spread lies. You know it's wrong, but you have two choices: you can either stand up for her and risk the group turning on you, too, or you can go along with the crowd because you want people to like you. Growing up, I saw that other kids were strong when they had the backup of their friends, but not when they were alone. They needed to be validated by others. And it's still like that. People get cheered on by the mob mentality. Let's gang up on someone! I doubt that girl who threw water at me in Minnesota would have done it if she was alone. Unfortunately, this mentality seems to be more prevalent than ever—especially in politics.

I will never apologize to anyone for being an independent thinker. Disagree with my politics, but don't tell me how to think and don't attack me personally. Don't say that I'm not smart enough to understand the issues. Don't tell me what I believe in and that I'm not conservative enough. I don't form my political beliefs based on acceptance by the self-appointed thought wardens of *either* political party and I never will. So you don't have to like or agree with my thoughts, but you should at least know that they are my own and you don't have to be a jerk about it. If you're pro-life and you want to have a conversation about why *Roe v. Wade* should be overturned, that's great because you're challenging my political beliefs. I'm all for healthy dialogue and debate. I'm not saying other women—especially other conservative women—have to agree with me. Just because you disagree with me on an issue doesn't mean you have to attack my looks and my intelligence. You don't have to "like" tweets and other social media posts that say I'm a stupid bimbo who is not good for the conservative movement. You're not coming at me with a true argument. Also, how can people who have never really met me tell me that I'm dumb just because I don't agree with them?

Make sure *you* are not a mean girl. There have been opportunities in my life when my enemies were down and it would have been really easy to kick them. Yet, you don't win by kicking people when they're down. (It's okay to kick an idea when it's down. That way it can't get back up.)

I don't care if someone is a liberal, conservative, an atheist, or whatever: don't be the mean girl. You may be in that position of power where you feel like you are controlling the room or you own the moment—whether that's at school, work, among your friends—but if you're a crappy person, it's worth nothing. Even when it's easy to be a mean girl, even when other people cheer you on for being one, don't do it. You won't be happy with yourself.

Chapter 4

NOBODY CARES.
WORK HARDER.

*Obsessed is a word the lazy use to
describe the dedicated.*

Many don't realize that one television minute is equivalent to about an hour of work. This is especially true for my commentaries. They may only be a few minutes long, but make no mistake, they are well thought out, meticulously written, and a true labor of love. They take time.

When I write "Final Thoughts," I comb through Twitter, Instagram, and several news websites to see what issues have people talking and what's trending. Some days it's easy—like the day after a Trump speech or a high school shooting. Those topics fire me up instantly and the speed of my fingertips on my keyboard could practically spark a fire. Other days it takes a bit longer. I have a rule: I will never write or comment on something that truly doesn't inspire me. If a celebrity makes a stupid comment about Trump and I don't care, I won't waste my time. The subject has to hit me. I have to feel something. I don't fake my anger, passion, or emotion. I couldn't. I'm not that good an actress.

After I finish writing my scripts, I send them in to the Fox News "brain room" for fact-checking. Believe me when I say that they don't allow fake news or alternative facts. You might not like what I'm saying or my opinion but I assure you—the facts check out. Once they give me the okay, I lock my dog in my room, head to my home studio, which is in the extra bedroom, and get to work. Yes, I am blessed to have a robo-cam in my home that is controlled and operated from New York. I put my earpiece in, enter my script into the prompter, and, wham-bam, it's time for "Final Thoughts."

Not long after I say, "God bless and take care," I'm back on my computer writing for the next day. But even that is far from the end of my workday, because I don't travel in a narrow lane. I've jackhammered this career path as wide as I can. Besides writing this book (another labor of love), I also work on long-form specials for Fox Nation. I want to tell the stories no other political talking head will tell. I want to hear from the wives of SEALs charged with war crimes. I want to talk to parents of a young man stabbed and murdered in Mexico. I want to spend time on the border with the agents. I have a list longer than a CVS receipt of all the interviews I want to do.

Now, that's all just in the normal workweek. My job doesn't end on Friday at 5 p.m. Not even close. I spend the majority of my weekends traveling the country giving speeches to a wide range of groups, from conservative Republican Lincoln Day dinners to the Black & Blue Ball to support the families of fallen police officers. I love doing my scripted commentaries, but these live speeches have my heart. There is nothing like walking onstage or to a podium knowing I have the opportunity to inspire the audience. Still, each and every time, I leave knowing that they have inspired me more than I could ever inspire them. They likely just don't know it.

All this is a lot of work, something many people don't realize. I get this sense when many girls tell me that they're making videos similar to my "Final Thoughts." "Do you think I can get in at Fox?" they ask me, or some variation of that. What people don't realize is the amount of work that goes into this *and* that I worked hard to get where I am. I didn't just make videos, post them online, and get a job at Fox. In college at UNLV, they had a political show called *The Scramble*. After making a name for myself as an outspoken, regular panelist during my junior and senior year, I was asked to host the show in the second semester of my senior year. I also hosted *two* shows before I even came to Fox: at One America, and at *The Blaze*. I put in the work and did anything and everything that I needed to, from booking my guests to writing my scripts. And I still do that now, even things that are technically not my job. When Fox Nation was launching, there were plenty of producers to send emails and reach out to possible guests. But you know what? I sent them myself because I know no one is going to work harder than I am. And that's the key! You've got to put in the work. It's not just going to happen for you, and if it *does* just happen for you it's going to be fleeting. You'll be a shooting star, not a sun. I think the problem with a lot of people—especially millennials—is that they don't want to put in the time and effort. They think they are going to be Kylie Jenner just because they like makeup or Erin Andrews because they like sports. So many people don't want to start at the bottom. They say, "I'm not where I want to be in my job, so I think I'm going to quit." But with that attitude, you're never going to get anywhere. You need to work your way up and do whatever you need to. You can't feel entitled and think you're supposed to make it without much effort. Sorry. That's just not going to happen.

The people who are willing to do anything are the ones who will succeed. My senior year of college, I applied for a postgraduation internship at *The Blaze*. They gave me every indication that I was going to get the job, so I was devastated when I was rejected. Really upset. But I gave myself five minutes to sulk, and then I thought, *What's my next move?* I googled conservative news outlets and found One America, a family-owned start-up in San Diego that was supposed to be an alternative to Fox. The first time I called them, they hung up. But I called back. I didn't give up, because often no one is going to help you and if you want to do something you have to do it yourself. Soon after that, when they finally agreed to meet me, I headed to San Diego for an interview. Although I'd never been to California, I put One America's address in my GPS and drove the five hours from Las Vegas in my 2008 Chevy Cobalt. I was nervous. I needed this internship. *But you've done everything you can*, I thought to myself. *You've worked as hard as possible. Now put it in God's hands and walk in there with confidence. If it's meant to be, it will be.*

My nerves disappeared the second I entered the office. That's the thing. If you walk into a building like you already own it, people pay attention. If you've done the work leading up to that moment, then you're prepared.

"I'll write for you. I'll get your coffee. I'll do anything," I told Mr. H, a man in his eighties who made his fortune selling vacuums and software. "Plus, I know politics inside and out, and I'm a 4.0 student. I just want to be a part of this."

"Let's do a screen test," he said. *I thought I was applying for an internship and now I'm doing a screen test to be an anchor?* Mr. H liked what he saw and offered me my own show. I tried to contain myself as I walked to the parking lot. *At twenty-one years old, I'm going to graduate from college and start my own show!* I was stunned, but I also knew that I had worked very hard to get to that point. Moreover, you rarely get hired for what you know and what you can do. Usually you're hired for what you're eager to find out.

It was a perfect match: One America was a start-up that needed a political talk show, and I had done election coverage and wrote, produced, and hosted a political roundtable show in college. Once I finished my classes, I packed my stuff and moved to San Diego. I didn't even walk in my college graduation ceremony, because I wanted to get to work. I was committed. Yes, graduation from college is a big day, but I see things bigger. I see things much further on the horizon. Try it. Think big. Be willing to do anything. Be willing to work harder than anyone else. I didn't know a soul in California, but I

pushed past my nerves. One America was a great opportunity. *I'll make friends later,* I thought.

WE LIVE IN a world where every kid gets a trophy just for
signing up for soccer, Little League, or whatever sport
because that's supposed to be "fair." But life's not fair!
So many parents clear away every obstacle for their kids
so they never have to deal with disappointment or failure. They handle all their problems. They are known as
"lawn mower parents." But nobody excels from that. En-
titlement is one of the biggest problems we face in society today, especially among young people. A lot of you
think you should get what you want simply because you
want it, that just by virtue of being born you get a trophy,
a gold star, and a free pass. Nope. Nobody cares what
you think you deserve. Get off your ass and work for it.
Does that hurt your feelings? Too bad. The pussification
of American youth has to stop.

I'll repeat it: Life. Is. Not. Fair. I'm tired of this thin-
skinned, poor-baby, don't-hurt-anyone's-feelings crap. That
was not how my parents raised me. Yes, they showered me
with love, and we are extremely close, but they didn't
baby me. They told me I wasn't better or worse than anyone else. "You're very special to *us*, but you're not special
to anybody else, so get out there and work hard," they

said. I think the world would be a much better place if other parents told their children the same thing. And if they told them the truth. *American Idol* was great when it first came out, before they whitewashed it and made it politically correct. Back then, Simon Cowell would tell someone flat out, "You're a terrible singer. You shouldn't do this. Don't quit your day job." Harsh? Maybe. But helpful? Definitely. I think the worst thing you can do is tell your kid that he is the best at something, especially when your kid sucks and his "dream" is *not* what he should be doing. Maybe it's a hobby, not a career path.

If you suck at something, either find a new path or work at it until you're the best. When I was in middle school, we had to do cartwheels in gym. The problem? I wasn't athletic—at all—and couldn't do one to save my life. It was horrible. So I went home and practiced that damn cartwheel every single day. I did it over and over and over. I set up a camcorder (that I worked to pay for myself) so I could watch what I was doing wrong and fix it. Why? I was not going to be embarrassed the next time I had to do a cartwheel in gym. Now, if my phys ed teacher had said, "Don't worry. It's okay. You don't have to do cartwheels," or if my parents told me how good I was at them, even though I sucked, what would that have done? Nothing. Absolutely nothing!

Parents are so worried about insulting their kids and

damaging their self-esteem. But disappointment and failures foster growth and success. You learn more from those things than you do from winning every time. If you're not the best at something, you should be motivated to do it better. And nothing hurts your self-esteem more than going into the real world and hearing for the first time that you're not the greatest or the best. On the other hand, nothing boosts your confidence more than working hard at something and then succeeding because you deserve it. Maybe that's why I am a conservative. I believe that, although the almighty (taxpayer funded) government can give you a lot of things, it can't give you self-worth or a sense of accomplishment. You have to earn that yourself. And guess what? It feels damn good. The common misconception about Republicans is that we don't care about poor people. Some people say we even hate them. Wrong. As a Republican, I want you to achieve for two reasons. One, the more people who earn their own way, the fewer my tax dollars pay to subsidize. Two, I want everyone to experience what a hard day's work feels like. I want you to go to sleep at night not just *feeling* like you've done something, but *knowing* damn well you did. Few things feel better than that!

Here's another harsh truth: no one cares about your excuses! *No one.* A year into my job at Fox, I was not where I wanted to be. I went from hosting a show five days a week on national TV to being on *Fox & Friends* once a week and doing videos for Fox News Insider. Was I happy about this? Not at all. Did I think I'd be doing more at that point in my career? Definitely. But did I blame someone else and make excuses? No. I just had to work harder, and I had to be patient. So even though it's my personality to get anxious, I have learned that timing is everything. I know things will happen the way they're supposed to and that I'm going to do an amazing job because I don't fail, I put in way more than 100 percent effort, and I have all the tools I need in my toolbox.

Everybody has obstacles in their life. Some have more, and some have less. But you can't blame a missed opportunity on another person or on people being mean to you. You can't blame it on your past. Don't let your results be a product of your excuses. Let them be a product of your blood, sweat, and tears! Go and make things happen. Because you *can* make them happen! The problem is that we often bitch and moan about obstacles and do everything we can to avoid them. Don't. Those obstacles have been placed in your path for a reason. Use them. Grow from them. Shatter them!

I won't do something half-assed, because I don't want someone looking at it and saying, "That's Tomi's work." If I'm going to do something, I want to be the best and have someone look at it and say, "*Oh my God!* That's

Tomi's work." This goes for anything and everything that I do. When I was selling jeans at Express, you'd better believe that I was the number one jean seller there. People would come in and say, "Is Tomi here?" I worked in retail throughout college. I would go to class, eat a peanut butter and jelly sandwich in my car, and then go to work. When I finally got off work around 10 p.m. (that was if assholes didn't come in two minutes before closing and ruin all the folded piles), I would go home and do my classwork. I'm not some special case. The most successful among us have done the same thing. So I'm going to do everything well because that builds character. That's what makes you stand out. Does minimum wage labor suck? Hell yes! That's why I worked my ass off in school: to make sure I would graduate with skills that would get me out of a minimum wage job that I hated. Ding! Ding! Ding! For those who whine about "a living wage," take note: if you're working a minimum wage job for years and haven't been promoted or elevated, chances are you're doing a shitty job, showing up late, or displaying a bad attitude.

I'm not going to have a bad attitude, because guess what? Whether people are watching you on TV or buying jeans from you, nobody cares even the tiniest bit that you're having a bad day. So you'd better put a smile on your face and deal with it. You're projecting what you want the world to think. If you're not where you want to be in life, don't sit there and complain. Ask yourself, are you *really* doing everything you can? Or are you holding back and phoning it in a little? Trust me, you're not fooling anyone. People can tell. Are you working hard? Or are you *talking* about how hard you work? Be honest with yourself. How badly do you want it? Because I can guarantee you that I want it more. I'm going to go above and beyond.

Approach everything with the idea that you're going to put your best self out there, whether it's a relationship, a job, encountering people you don't know, or anything else. When I go give a speech, I put as much work into it whether I'm being paid $15,000 or am doing it for free. And I'm still going to take hundreds of pictures after it's over, because that's how people remember you. When I look myself in the mirror, I ask: *What did I do today to get me closer to what I want to achieve?* Think of it this way: today twenty-four hours are going to go by regardless of whether or not you seize them. You can get up and let them slip through your fingers, *or* you can make the most of the time that God has given you on this earth. That's what I do every day. What am I going to do to get myself closer to my goal and where I want to be? That's why losing my job at *The Blaze* was so hard: I felt like I was being held back by forces outside my control. I saw the destination, but I couldn't move toward it because of all this legal stuff, and I couldn't do what I wanted to do anymore. It's difficult when someone else takes control of your destiny. So take control rather than being passive.

Why? Because victimhood is not cute. I promise that you're never going to say, "I felt like a victim today and achieved my dreams." No one has ever accomplished anything waiting for a handout. You can't sit there and think, *I hope someone gives me an amazing opportunity today.* It's like sitting on the couch waiting for Mr. Right to break into your house. It's not going to happen. You have to put in the effort. And even if you have to work a little harder than anyone else you know, don't focus on that. Don't waste your time telling people how hard you work. Just do it, and they'll see. Unfortunately, there will be people all around you telling you that you can't. You can't wear that. You can't say that. You can't talk like that. Can't, can't, can't. What to do? Turn around and say, "Watch me." Don't let anyone dim your light just because it's shining in their eyes. Yes, I had Glenn Beck screaming in my face at *The Blaze*, but I didn't let that diminish me. Instead I worked harder.

One day in the middle of my show, I saw the makeup artist standing on the side waving at me. When we went to break, she ran over to me with a Kleenex.

"Beth said you have glitter on your face and we have to wipe it off, or you can't finish your show," she said. Beth was a member of the FOG (friends of Glenn), one of his minions who did all his bidding at the time.

"I'm not wearing glitter. It's probably just eye shadow that dropped," I said.

"They said you have to take it off."

"I have a full face of makeup. If I wipe one spot, it will all come off," I said. The supposed piece of glitter stayed put, and so did I. But that wasn't the end of it. After the show, I got called up to Human Resources to talk about the glitter on my face. *Are you kidding me?* I thought.

Another time it was the middle of the show when my producer Jessica started talking in my earpiece.

"We're going to pan the camera, and someone is going to come over and take your space heater," she said, referring to the one I used because Glenn insisted that the studio be kept at 55 degrees. You couldn't even see the heater on camera because it was under my desk, but sure enough someone came running out and took it.

"What was that about?" I asked Jessica after the show. Ellen, Glenn's right-hand woman, came in and said, "If the space heater is not moved in thirty seconds, every one of you is going to be fired as per Glenn." Can you imagine that they were going to fire the whole control room and my producers if my space heater was not removed? These incidents were constant. They were trying to do anything they could to make my life miserable.

Glenn and his FOG tried to hamper my team at every turn. Instead of giving us offices, they made us sit in the middle of the room. Instead of being helpful, they were rude. But we just kept our heads down and stayed focused on the big picture. And guess what? We excelled! Every time they would try to water us down, we would keep growing and growing. We didn't mope around saying, "They don't like us here." We thought, *They don't like us here? I guess we'll have to work harder.* And let's be honest, none of my viewers cared about any of that. They didn't care that I had to fight to get things done and that I had to work harder than anyone else in the building. They cared about the final product: my show. I still do more than I need to do at Fox because no one is going to work harder than I will. Yes, you need to learn to trust your team and give people tasks, but nobody is going to look out for you like *you* are going to look out for you, so make sure that you're paying attention and controlling your destiny. If I go on Fox and I do something that's substandard, nobody is going to think about the five people who worked on it with me. They're only going to see that I did something substandard. So you'd better believe I'm going to make sure that it's great. That's my name on the line.

Keep moving forward and seeing the big picture. When something bad happens, sitting back and feeling sorry for yourself is not going to do a damn thing. Feel sorry for yourself for five minutes and then get your shit together. Move on and figure out what you're going to do next. That's what I had to do when I left One America and when I was suspended from *The Blaze*. *Yeah, I'm fired. It sucks. Now what am I going to do?* That's what I had to do when I got cheated on and dumped. It's okay to fall because it just makes your chin stronger. (Mine is stronger than ever, which it needs to be to support my sassy mouth.) But pick yourself up.

There is no time to feel sorry for yourself because the world is going to keep spinning. No one cares that your life is not perfect right now, so what are you going to do? How are you going to make it okay? How are you going to live with yourself? Often the next step is doing something scary. And you know what I say: if something scares you, run toward it as fast as you can. You don't know what the future holds; none of us do. But isn't that exciting? The exceptional never fear change, they embrace it. Even when I didn't have a job, I shot "Final Thoughts" from my car with terrible audio. I did the best I could and it worked. My "Final Thoughts" on transgender in the military got 25 million views. Yep. Twenty-five million! From my car! There's a quote I've seen that says, "When one door closes, sometimes you want to get a hammer and nails to make sure that bitch stays shut." So nail it shut and go onward and upward.

Also, part of working toward what you want is how you treat other people. Be kind to everyone—those who are above you, those who are below you, everyone. Trust me, people will remember how you act and how you make them feel. Treat them with respect. I always thank anyone I work with and tell them I appreciate *their* hard work, because I do. I see people in my industry whose heads swell to three times their original size. They think they only need to be nice to people who can give them something and they're mean to people who can't. I say be nice to them all. Why wouldn't I be? That's how my parents raised me. I don't get any joy out of being a nasty person or ungrateful. Recently a total stranger FedEx'd me a bag of shit. Yes, you read that correctly. Real live poop! For no reason. Why would someone waste their time and money on being that mean? Just imagine what they could do if they channeled all that energy into working hard.

I learned this life-changing value from my family. They taught me through their example. My mom's dad, Grandpa Dietrich, had just an eighth-grade education, yet he built a multimillion-dollar ranch from nothing. When my dad's dad, Grandpa Lahren, lost both of his parents at the age of thirteen, he started driving a truck to earn money. After fighting in World War II as a Marine Corps paratrooper, he ranched during the day and railroaded at night. My point is that my grandparents didn't make excuses. They never said, "Poor me," and they taught their families to do the same. Chances are, your grandparents did the same. My parents are the hardest-working people I know. They always go forth and take it on. Growing up, we had enough money, but we were never rich (despite what some naïve people say about me on social media). My parents drove their cars until they fell apart and we went on just two or three family vacations my whole life. My mom clipped coupons and both my parents were really careful with their spending. They still are.

For twenty-six years, my dad loved his job as the shipping supervisor at a particleboard plant. That is, until the company got bought out and his new bosses treated everyone like dirt. They would call him in on weekends to perform jobs that were far below his pay grade for no reason other than to bully and belittle. They also seemed to want him to undercut other vendors, and when he wouldn't do it, they would insult and harass him. Then my dad found out that he was being replaced by a man whom *he* had trained because they could pay the other guy less. After my dad spent decades on the job and ascended to a well-deserved management position, his new bosses were going to put him back on the night shift and on the floor. Or so they thought! My dad quit on the spot. He didn't know what he was going to do, but he certainly wasn't going to be belittled. Sacrificing his self-esteem was not worth it. Still, he didn't mope around wishing for a job. From the second he quit, he was out there looking, willing to work for less money or try something new, which is exactly what happened when my dad found Target Corporation. There he wasn't doing what he had for almost three de- cades, but he gave it his all. He always says, "Anything worth doing is worth doing right." No matter how tired he is, he goes into work with a positive attitude and thinking, What could I do to be better?

My dad doesn't just clock in and out. When he comes home at night, he continues working hard. He'll order items on eBay with his own money that he thinks can help the company. Why? Because he's going to be the best. Always. Growing up, he did everything around our house, and if something wasn't perfect, he'd start again. When he fenced our property, he redid an entire section because the wires weren't as tight as he wanted. Every- body else thought they looked great, but it wasn't up to his standards. "I have to look at that every day," he said.

My father always goes above and beyond, and he's not the only one. When I was in high school, there was a point when my mom worked two jobs so that we could afford the clothes and other things I needed. She'd come home from a long day at work, put on a T-shirt, and work as a waitress in a loud, smoky bar. And the woman is hard of hearing! Even with hearing aids, it's difficult, and yet she did it. Then she'd come home, go to sleep, and wake up early to go back to her first job. On weekends she cleaned the house and caught up on personal errands. She didn't complain that she couldn't hear people or that she was tired after a long day's work, she just did it. That's inspiring to me. My parents talk about being proud of me, but what they don't realize is that I'm where I am because of their example.

My mom is the youngest of three children. Tracy is her older sister and Todd her older brother. Growing up, my parents never had the money that her siblings had, and their two families would compete back and forth. Tracy would get a new car, so then Todd would get a new car. Todd would renovate his house, so Tracy would renovate her house. And there we were: my mom, dad, and I lived in the same house my whole life. In fact, they still live there and have the same refrigerator they had when I was born! My parents don't buy new couches, but instead get those that are refurbished, and they drive their vehicles for years and years. They never say, "I wish I could drive a new car," or, "I want a remodeled house like everybody else." My aunts, uncles, and cousins went on fancy vacations; we didn't. That's not what we valued. However, it always seemed like my mom's siblings looked down on her and our family because my mom didn't have a fancy job and my parents didn't make as much money.

Unfortunately, it affected my mom's self-esteem. She always thinks that her sister and sister-in-law are prettier and skinnier than her and have more money than her. She's so tough on herself. I've tried to help her feel better by saying things like, "Mom, look at our family. You, Dad, and I are so close, and you and Dad have been married for thirty-six years while your sister is divorced and remarried." My aunt's husband is a great guy, but my parents are the happiest couple I've ever seen. And while my cousins were partying and doing other things, I never got in trouble. "Don't feel inferior because they have more money," I would tell her. Now I think she finally gets to brag about me, and they hate that. She doesn't rub it in their faces at all, but says things subtly and simply. "Trump tweeted about Tomi," she'll tell them. Still, they hate it because I think they have always underestimated my mom. Don't you see that everything comes back in life? Just live your life and it will come back. Stay laser focused and you will succeed. My parents kept their heads down and worked hard. They did a lot with nothing. So can you! Yes, *you!* My parents were grateful for what they already had and taught me to be the same way, because someone somewhere is praying for the things you take for granted.

Bottom line? We have a finite amount of time on this earth, so if you're going to do something, why be mediocre? Instead use your twenty-four hours a day, seven days a week to get it. Grind hard. Love hard. Get on your knees to thank God for all you have and to pray, then get on your feet to work hard.

Chapter 5

"LIKE" YOURSELF.

*I stopped worrying about losing fans a long time
ago. I'm far more concerned with losing myself
trying to please the people around me.*

I use social media. I love social media. It's a business tool
for me, but I've found that if you use it for validation, you
become a tool. I have 1.5 million followers on Instagram,
and I can get 100,000 "likes" on a picture, but I have just
five close friends.

I have 4.6 million Facebook followers, but when I'm
not on the road, I come home every night to my rescue
chihuahua, Kota. (Humans will disappoint you. That's
why God created dogs.) My rise and fall won't be dictated by Twitter, what people say about me, or how many

followers I have. Yes, these things *are* important because it's my brand, but I can tell you that "likes" and followers are not my life. That's not where my self-worth comes from. Social media is a blessing and a curse—even for me. Sure, I've built a brand and a following on social media, and in some ways these people are my family. They are at the very least my focus group. I wouldn't be living my dream on Fox News if it weren't for the loyal fans, followers, and even haters who propelled me to this place. *However*, social media has become an addiction, and I'll admit that I was an addict.

Do you ever realize how bad it is? Be honest, because it can become an obsession. When you're sitting at a red light for even a minute, do you reach for your phone? Do you check your "likes" or read your comments section? I did. When you're at dinner with family or friends, is your phone next to your water glass? Are you itching to check it? I was. When you're at a concert, are you watching it through your eyeballs or your phone's camera so you can post it on your story? When Instagram and Facebook went down for less than a day in March 2019, did you feel like you lost an appendage? I admit, I did. It's okay to love social media but remember: it's a thing, not a person. Don't obsess over it. Problem is, we've grown to love things and use people when it should be the other way around. I remind myself of this daily.

Our culture has become so obsessed with fame and infamy, we're willing to do anything so people will see us on social media, the Internet, and the news. Is that the point we've come to now? We do things just to be the center of attention? Even horrible, disgusting things? One example: Months after the Parkland, Florida, school shooting, it was revealed that the shooter made videos on his cell phone that showed him talking about how many people he was going to kill. Yes. This is a very extreme story, but there are some people who become famous for what they do, and there are some people who do what they do to *become* famous. Don't be one of those people.

Life is not about retweets, Google alerts, followers, haters, or copycats. Life is about the people who keep you grounded and remind you that none of that shit matters. I can read 100 comments about how I'm pretty, and I can read 300 about how I'm an ugly ogre, but I try really hard not to let *any* of them affect me and you shouldn't, either. Validation doesn't come from Instagram. It doesn't come from Facebook, Twitter, or page views. It doesn't come from being homecoming queen or the most popular girl in your high school or college. My dad once told me, "Life is not about fame and money. I've never gone to a funeral where I saw somebody pull up with a truckload of money." True. And when you're dead, I'm pretty sure people aren't going to mention your Instagram followers in their eulogies.

What I will always be is true to myself and my voice. I've been shunned, labeled, and ridiculed for that voice by both the left and the right! Yet I carry on and I don't apologize for it. You can call me a lot of things, but a bandwagoner isn't one of them. I choose to be honest and authentic over perfect every single time. And I think it's that authenticity that has led to much of my success. I know that I work in a crowded industry and that I'm not the smartest, prettiest, or most experienced political commentator out there, but I don't need to be. It's my gut instincts that have given me staying power. That's true of all people with staying power. Sometimes we make mistakes and do the wrong thing, but not because we followed the crowd.

When I post pictures with my boyfriend, people make comments like "Unfollow her" or "You'd get more followers if you didn't post about your boyfriend." I am going to be honest. At first I was wary of this, thinking that seeing Brandon would turn guys off and affect my brand. But I'm not going to avoid posting about someone who is in my life and whom I love, just because I might lose male followers. Not only that. I want to show girls what a good, healthy relationship looks like. My close followers comment that I look so happy. They can see this and they respond to it because it's real. I'm far less concerned about losing guy followers than I am about inspiring young girls and letting people see the real side of me. If I make a political post, I get many fewer likes because people can see my political commentary in other places. I think the reason I have more Instagram followers, hands down, than anyone else at Fox is that I let people into my life. I let them see me just being me and they see that I'm not angry all the time. I'm not talking about politics all the time, either. I have a life that includes friends, family, and fun. In many ways, I'm just like them. I'm successful because I don't use Instagram as a life guide. I use it so people can get to know me.

Twitter and Instagram are not everything, but you can easily get sucked into thinking social media is the whole world. It's mind-boggling that people sit behind their computers—hiding, actually—and take the time to say nasty things about others. It happens to me all the time, and they don't even know me. Most of the time I don't respond. Although recently I couldn't help it. A friend posted a picture of us at a fashion show.

"How could you be seen with her. She's so disgusting and vile?" someone wrote. So I responded: "Hi John. Sorry that you feel that way. I don't think we've ever met. Have we?" But I don't live on Twitter. I am not a one-dimensional person. I have a great house, family, boyfriend, and dog. I live fully every single day. And if I delete my Twitter app right now, is that going to dictate my family? Is that going to dictate the beautiful afternoon I'm going to have? Is that going to dictate the truly good people around me? No. I try to compartmentalize it and remember that I use social media for business, not for validation, and not to boost my confidence or self-esteem.

All this leads me to the important topic of confidence. People always say things to me like "I bet you were homecoming queen in high school or a cheerleader." Nope. Not even close. I wasn't an athlete. I wasn't a dancer. I wasn't in the band. I wasn't popular. I was interested in politics, which is not the coolest topic when you're a teenager. But I always had confidence, which is why the question I get most often *isn't* political. It's "How do you have confidence?"

To me, confidence isn't about walking into the room and being the prettiest girl or the smartest girl; it's about being the one who lights up the room. You're not seeking approval from anyone else. Even if you're not feeling that way in the moment, you've got to hype yourself up. I tell myself, I'm going to walk into this room, and I'm going to own it. I remember driving that five hours from Las Vegas to San Diego to interview for an internship at One America just a month before I was supposed to graduate from college. I was nervous. Like I said, I *needed* the job.

But I walked in there like I already owned the building and told them I could do anything they asked. I once read this quote, "I know what I bring to the table, so I'm not afraid to eat alone." It's true. I know what I'm bringing so I walk in with confidence. Confidence isn't something that you have because you are the best or because you feel like the best. Confidence is when you're *not* feeling your best, but you're going to go out and be your best *anyway*. Act like a queen even if you don't feel like a princess. It's about being strong and making yourself feel empowered even on the days when you don't feel like it. Even on the days when you don't look cute. Even on the days when you get dumped or fired (been there, done both). Even on the days when people are mean to you on Instagram (happens all the time). Confidence is when you think, I feel weak today but I'm going to be strong. It's walking into any room and saying, "I might not be the brightest, the richest, the funniest, or the most athletic. I might not be the most well-spoken, but I know who I am and I'm proud of that because I'm a good person." Stand tall and remember who the fuck you are.

I have had my fair share of social media "feuds." I've been threatened by the rapper Cardi B, attacked by the rapper Nicki Minaj. Come to think of it, I've been attacked by the rap community and its fans. Strangely, I am used to it. But there was one particularly vile rapper—I use the word "rapper" very loosely because he hasn't really been relevant in ten years—who calls himself "The Game." His degrading posts on social media about me were so below the belt, sexually explicit, and vulgar that I hesitated to respond at first.

See, I have no problem arguing political points or policy but this fool's attack on me had nothing to do with politics. It was all personal, all disgusting, and—yes, dare I say it—sexist? I do. Sexist!

The things he said about me were perhaps the ugliest and most repulsive things I have ever read.

And I've read A LOT of nasty things about myself. He kisses his daughter with that mouth, and that's also troubling. He posted an Instagram photo of me with a caption so nasty and so horrific it doesn't deserve space in my book. He then posted an unflattering photo of me from high school and joked about how ugly I was and how I had plastic surgery (I didn't).

I was about sixteen years old in the photo and yep, it's an ugly photo of me, but *still*, I'm proud of it.

Why? Because guess where that photo was from— an article in my local newspaper about getting a summer job.

I have thick skin, really thick skin, but I am still a human being. I am someone's daughter, someone's granddaughter, someone's girlfriend, and a person. You don't have to like me. You can even call me ugly, dumb, or a whole dictionary full of horrible things, but the collection of things that have been said or directed at me from The Game and friends is not okay. And it's not just that it's not okay to say those things to me . . . It's not okay, period. That is why I posted that high school photo he mocked on my Instagram for the world to see. I will not let someone's sick and twisted words go to my heart.

Look, I don't worry about me. I signed up for this.

I think about all the young ladies who follow me and read this stuff and see this stuff.

The Game took it a step further and defended his repulsive behavior on the day-time talk show *The Real*, saying, "It's never a woman thing. That post was about Tomi Lahren herself for her actions, and I wanted to post something and be brash about it, and I hope that it made her day bad, and her coworkers looked at her crazy, and she had a terrible day."

Not only is what he said about me disgusting, explicit, and wrong, but I know girls see this stuff and think, *I will never speak out like Tomi does and I will never be confident in my opinions because look what happens when you are—you get treated like less than a human.* And to attack my appearance when I was in high school, really?

Where are the feminists? Since when has that been okay? Just because I'm Tomi?

Girls struggle enough with personal confidence and self-esteem and when they see rappers with millions of followers attack someone's appearance—what message does that send?

Well, ladies, I hope you know that I will be okay. I will fight on.

I will *not* be silenced or intimidated by the filth that is hurled at me by low-class rappers.

And I know not all of you want this kind of public life, and I don't blame you.

I just hope, in your own life, that you are strong enough to block out hate like this.

You will likely not experience it on the level I do, and I'm glad. But you will experience it in some way, shape, or form—especially if you're a conservative and choose to be vocal and proud of it.

I don't back down and I don't stoop to their level because that's not how I was raised.

I may make political points that offend people and I'll own that, but I would never even *think* half of the things that are said about me and to me. I wouldn't wish that kind of language on my worst enemy.

"Likes" and retweets are not the real world. If you get your joy from that, you need to reexamine *why*. For example, how many times has this happened: You have one hundred comments on a post, saying you're gorgeous, you're beautiful, you're so cool, etc. But then one person says you're ugly and all of a sudden it's like, "I'm ugly," and your confidence plummets. Why? Because we put much more weight into the negative than we do the positive.

I love reality TV—especially *Keeping Up with the Kardashians.* On one episode, Kim realized that someone took a picture of her at the beach that showed her cellulite and posted it on social media. She was devastated. She literally didn't want to go out of the house! She didn't want to go to the Met Gala because she didn't want people to talk about her and she worried about how she should stand so others couldn't see the cellulite. This is *Kim Kardashian,* of all people! This is someone who posts hundreds of pictures of herself a week, poses naked, and loves herself. She's on the cover of magazines. She's rich, famous, and pretty. Millions of people love her. Many want to *be* her. With all this, you would think she'd be the most confident woman, that she wouldn't give a crap what anyone said about her looks. Yet Kim was sitting there looking at tagged photos of herself on Instagram and having a mental breakdown because some person in Bumfuck, Idaho, told her she had cellulite. She's had thousands of gorgeous photos taken of her, but *one* bad picture left her feeling so insecure and horrible. Why? Because a lot of her confidence is based on what other people think of her on social media.

My point is this: when people are mean to you or criticize you, don't let it go to your heart, and when people are sweet, nice, and complimentary, don't let it go to your head. You have to take *both* with a grain of salt. I don't get my confidence from reading Twitter or Instagram comments where people tell me I'm beautiful. If I did, then what would happen on the many, many, *many* days when people make fun of my nose and tell me that I have a huge forehead and big thighs? I wouldn't get out of bed!

When I say "like" yourself, I mean that if the validation of others dictates your confidence, that's not confidence. You are letting other people control what you think about yourself, and the problem is that when you put your happiness in the hands of someone else, you're never going to be happy. That's why people get into bad relationships or take jobs they hate: because everything is dictated by how someone *else* feels about them. You date a guy because he tells you that you're pretty and that you're great and you seek that validation. But when he dumps you, you feel like crap about yourself. Or you take a job where the boss thinks you're a star, but when he belittles you, you doubt yourself and your self-esteem plummets. This not only affects your work but every aspect of your life. This could have happened to me at One America, but luckily I had the confidence to withstand the storm of a moody, unconventional boss. After about six months at One America, *On Point with Tomi Lahren* grew in popularity, moving to two shows per week. More and more important people were watching it, including the organizers of the Conservative Political Action Conference (CPAC) 2014, who invited me to give a speech that February. I was thrilled.

"I hear about these typical Republicans being old, rich, white men," I said in my speech. "Well, look at the Democrats. You've got Hillary, Joe Biden, and Elizabeth Warren. Old, rich, white and, if the pantsuit fits, male, too." It got a lot of laughs, but its impact went beyond the conference audience when it went viral. Why? Because I went *there*. I was this unknown young girl giving a speech during the worst time slot at CPAC—9:30 a.m.—but I made a joke that no one else would make. Did I call Hillary and Elizabeth Warren men? Yeah, I did. Get over it.

After that *On Point with Tomi Lahren* became One America's top show, moving to five times a week. I was on a high note. "Final Thoughts" was also gaining popularity, so we put those segments on YouTube. But it wasn't until I did "Final Thoughts" on the Chattanooga, Tennessee, shooting of four United States marines in July 2015 that the numbers skyrocketed. It got 5 million views by the following afternoon. As my ratings continued to rise and I received more and more requests for appearances, my boss, Mr. H, asked me to sign a three-year contract. It increased my salary but prohibited me from going on other networks or radio shows and writing books. I stalled Mr. H for weeks, but finally, he called me into his office.

"You need to sign this," he said.

"Mr. H, I can't sign a three-year contract if you won't allow me to do anything else."

"You're just a dumb bimbo," he said. "If you won't sign it, you're done." I was shocked.

"Okay. I'll finish my show and leave," I told him. And I did. I gritted my teeth and held it together for the last time. There's that expression about stiffening your upper lip to get through tough moments. But one thing I've learned is that sometimes you have to take that literally—especially when you are upset but don't want to show outward vulnerability. At that moment with Mr. H (or later, when Glenn Beck was yelling in my face), I had to physically stiffen my upper lip and throw my shoulders back with confidence. I told myself, *This will not shake you. You might walk out of here and break down, but you're going to wait until you're alone or with people who truly care about you.*

Then I packed up my office and left ASAP. I could have easily signed that contract and been at One America for three years. After all, the pay was decent for a twenty-two-year-old; my then-boyfriend was based in San Diego and so were all my friends. That would have been easy, but it wouldn't have been right. This was God saying, "It's transition time. You got what you could from this experience and here's the next adventure." And you've got to have the faith and confidence to move forward. I am my biggest critic *and* my biggest challenger. I'm un-fuck-withable.

I was upset, but deep down I knew that a network did not make me and a network could not break me. Nobody wrote for me. Nobody did the work for me. So unless they were going to take my brain away, they couldn't stop me. Of course, I know there are women who can't just walk away from a job because they need it so they can feed their kids. And I understand that.

However, in the long run you will only succeed by following your inner compass. If you need to keep walking in the wrong direction to get that paycheck, keep looking for the right job. Because you're going to have to go a long way around to get back on the right track.

My next step after One America took even more confidence: I moved my whole life to Dallas for *The Blaze*. I said good-bye to my boyfriend and friends, broke my lease, and packed up my apartment, again moving to a place where I didn't know a soul. Still, I was thrilled about being at *The Blaze*. *This isn't going to be like One*

America with my boss calling me a bimbo, I thought. *This place is different.* Though *The Blaze* told me that I had to move to Dallas immediately, I arrived to find that I had no producers, no set, no show, nothing. To me, part of being un-fuck-withable is working hard even if no one is going to help you. You need to find it within yourself to make it happen.

That is why I wrote several sample shows so *The Blaze* could see what mine would look like. But this didn't matter to them. The start date kept changing. I continued to bring them ideas, but they were constantly pushing me to the side. Their excuses kept coming. I was furious. But I was also confident enough to push back, because life is too short to be miserable. So I asked myself, *What can I do better? Am I going to live my life or live my best life?* It doesn't mean it's going to come easy, quickly, or without disappointment. You're probably going to fail. Get over it. Get on your knees and pray, then get on your feet and work. So that's what I continued to do.

"Can I at least do my 'Final Thoughts' on Facebook?" I asked. If they wouldn't put me on TV, this was my only means to get to the people. The producers just wanted to get me out of their hair, so they said, "Yes." I wrote "Final Thoughts" from my windowless dressing room and filmed them from the hallway. As soon as I posted them, they started hitting millions. The one I did on the San Bernardino terrorist attack got 17 million hits in two days. Why? Because it was authentic and I said what everyone was thinking: I went full roar, and I wasn't afraid to say "radical Muslims." I was very direct and passionate, and people recognized that and appreciated it. In fact, that's what many people wrote in their comments to me. They said, "That's what I was thinking. But I didn't say it." When I talk about immigration in "Final Thoughts," I'm not afraid to say, "I'm tired of pressing 'two' for English." Many Americans feel that way, but they can't say it because they think someone will take it as racist. But I don't care. These thoughts may be politically incorrect, but they're intellectually honest. Soon enough, my "Final Thoughts" reached more people on a nightly basis than *The Blaze* did in a year. They had about 25,000 subscribers; I would get 25,000 comments on one video.

In January, I had a meeting about my show. When I arrived, everyone was there except Glenn.

"Guys, it's been five months. Why isn't my show ready?" I asked. "You're running promos saying that it's starting, but it's not."

"We're going through a transition," said one of Glenn's lackeys. "We're not ready."

"But *I'm* ready," I said. "I've been writing sample

shows and taping them for nothing. I have been doing
'Final Thoughts,' and they're hitting millions. What's going on?" At that moment, Glenn stormed into the room.

"We don't just put shit on the air. When I say it's ready,
it's ready!" he screamed as he stood above me. His face
was bright red like I'd never seen. With the kind of anger
he had, you would have thought that I had set the building
on fire. This was only the second time I'd ever talked to
him. I was so confused. Here I was *asking* to work, telling them that I didn't want to sit there and get paid to do
nothing, and he was yelling at me?

Finally, they told me that February 2 was the new start
date for my show, with one a week even though my contract was for four. But what else could I do besides make
the best of it? My second show was right after the Super
Bowl and thanks to my "Final Thoughts" about Beyoncé's
halftime performance, my ratings blew up, and my Facebook views skyrocketed. Still, *The Blaze* criticized me for
everything. A month before the election, Glenn went on an
anti-Trump Facebook rant saying Hillary was the "moral
and ethical choice." He *didn't* endorse her, but the media
twisted his words to say that he did. Everyone kept tweeting me things like "You're not going to be able to support Trump anymore because Glenn supports Hillary" or
"Glenn hates Trump." I tweeted back what I thought was a
very professional response:

"Glenn can endorse anyone he wants. Luckily, my network allows me to think for myself." I was giving *The Blaze* credit for having different opinions, but no.

The next day, I had just finished one show and was in the middle of an interview with the *Dallas Morning News*.

"Tomi, can I talk to you for a second?" Glenn called from his office. I knew something was up because Glenn wouldn't normally talk to me. He treated me like vapor.

"Sure," I said. His was an all-glass office, so the reporter from the *Dallas Morning News* was standing out there watching us, as was my producer.

"The next time you're going to tweet about something, have the decency to check if it's correct!" he screamed in my face, his cheeks turning redder and redder. He looked like he was going to explode.

"What?"

"You tweeted that I endorsed Hillary."

"No. I didn't. I said that our network allows us to think differently. I'm sorry."

The Blaze claimed it was a place for all voices, which is what I was trying to say with my response. I was on *their* team.

"Well, next time you better get it right," he said, turning around and storming into his inner sanctum, then slamming the door in my face. I was mortified. I couldn't believe a grown man freaked out over an innocent tweet. How could a twenty-four-year-old be more mature and dignified than the man *Time* magazine named as one of the "100 Most Influential" in 2010?

Having confidence also gets you through potentially tricky moments. Last year at Politicon, when I was walking out onto the stage with Chelsea Handler, I was a bit nervous. After all, this is someone I watched on TV every night in high school, and I also knew that I was heading into potentially unfriendly territory. The same thing happened when I was asked to go on *The Daily Show with Trevor Noah*.

In September 2016, Trevor dedicated his monologue to me in a spoof of my "Final Thoughts." At the end, he superimposed himself next to me on the set of my show on *The Blaze* with a bouquet of flowers. Sure, he was making fun of me but I loved every minute of it. It was tasteful and funny and I have no problem laughing at myself. A few weeks later, his team reached out to book me on *The Daily Show with Trevor Noah*. Well, duh, of course I agreed! People in my conservative media circle thought I was nuts to go on the show. They told me it would be an attack, but I didn't listen. Quite frankly, I had been attacked so frequently at that point that it was water off a duck's back.

I flew to New York City with my then-producer at *The*

Blaze (and current best friend), Jessica. She wasn't going to miss what would be a huge milestone in my career! Earlier on the day of the show, I met with a *New York Times* writer who was working on a profile piece about me. I invited him along to the show taping that night. I wasn't worried. The producers had called me more than once insisting it was to be a lighthearted segment. We were supposed to laugh and joke and Trevor had no intention of making me a punching bag. I believed them.

Before the show started, Trevor stopped by the green-room to greet me. *How nice*, I thought. "Hosts rarely do that," Jessica told me. I was feeling good backstage until I heard what Trevor set up when he addressed his audience to introduce me, "Imagine you're at Thanksgiving and your racist uncle walks in." *What happened to fun and lighthearted?* Then the second I walked onto the stage Trevor said, "Why are you so angry?" Though I was caught off guard, I rolled with the punches. He did everything in his power to bait me into saying something racist, all the while encouraging the audience to laugh at my expense.

PEOPLE THINK I'M racist because they think you can't talk about race if you're white. That's bullshit. I can talk about whatever the hell I want to. We can't sort anything out if we can't get our cards on the table. Pointing things out doesn't make you a racist if they're true.

Beyond that, I talk about Hillary Clinton often, and she is as white as they get. I've gone after John McCain and Jeff Flake, two white Republicans, and Elizabeth Warren, the fake Native American. I don't pick and choose my arguments based on someone's race or gender. Trevor Noah knew I wasn't a racist, but he put up this persona to play for his "team." What's funny is that he texted me randomly for months after his show, addressing me as "beautiful" and asking how I was doing. Then he'd go on a radio show like *The Breakfast Club* and imply that I'm racist. Nice. Really nice.

But I don't let things like that shake me, because I have confidence. I know what I'm doing. Yes, when I come to a table, I might be twenty-six years old, blond, and female, and everybody sitting around me may be twice my age and with twice as much experience. And most are male. But why let that intimidate me? I'm sitting elbow to elbow with these people and have accomplished what they have at half their age. I'm no less than they are. You may not be going on TV or getting booed, but maybe you're nervous walking into a meeting, job interview, or date. Don't be. Instead, remind yourself that this could be a moment that's going to change your life. Own it and embrace it. Fake the confidence if you don't have it, because the more you do it, the easier it becomes.

Of course, I don't always feel strong. Thanks to a few recent incidents—getting asked to leave a restaurant and people trying to trip me at a bar, to name just a few—I've become a little wary in big groups. A few months ago, I was out at a beach bar with friends. As I walked to the bathroom, I saw a couple of people looking at me. I crouched down and hid my face under my hat. I didn't want to be noticed. A few minutes passed, and I thought to myself, *Tomi, what the hell are you doing? Square your shoulders, stand up and walk out there.* And I did. Why would I sit there and let other people make me feel like I have to hide? We hear it all the time: how you talk to yourself matters. Having that strong inner voice helps you build yourself up and condition yourself to be a confident person. And that's what you're going to project to the world. But if you always doubt yourself in your mind, you won't.

Every time I start to doubt myself, feel uncomfortable, or think that maybe I'm not good enough or that people hate me, I ask myself: *Why?* Why are you allowing other people to suck your energy? Why would you allow them to ruin your day, your attitude, or your mood? You can't. I am a firm believer that you *choose* your mood. If you choose to be in a bad mood, you'll be in a bad mood.

If you choose to be in a good mood, you'll be in a good mood. You get that choice every single day when you wake up. So ask yourself, Am I going to be in a good mood today? Am I going to take what life throws at me today or am I going to act like a victim? Am I going to be my true self?

Being yourself is when you get to the point where you don't need to impress anybody. You can be authentically happy with who you are. I like people who don't care if people like them. Those are the people I want to be friends with. And it's not because they are rude, mean, or coldhearted. Not at all. It's because they don't care what the *outer* circle thinks of them because they know their *inner* circle thinks a lot of them. I pray you quit over-thinking, replaying failed scenarios, feeding self-doubt, beating yourself up, and seeing the beauty in everyone but yourself. You deserve more. Two important parts of being yourself are 1) never apologizing for the truth and 2) always apologizing when you're wrong.

Part of not apologizing for the truth is not apologizing for who you are, and that's what Trump does. Trump is a street fighter. He doesn't pull punches. He doesn't back down. He doesn't sugarcoat things. He doesn't try to please this group or that. During his campaign, Trump didn't need the Republican National Committee's money, so he didn't play to that crowd. Trump won because he's not a traditional Republican. He didn't need to play to a team. He plays for the American people.

Other Republicans, however, lose every time they stop standing up for themselves. They bow to the left and let them set the rules of the game. John McCain was the first candidate I supported, even though I was too young to vote in the 2008 election, and Mitt Romney was the first candidate I voted for, so I watched both of those elections very closely. Why did they lose? Because they apologized! Both Romney and McCain apologized for being Republican, they apologized for being conservative, they apologized for being white, and they apologized for being men. Don't apologize for the truth, which also means that you don't back down if you know that your intentions are honest and pure. Take the Kardashians, for example. (Yes, I love reality TV and try to get something out of every situation!) Right now I'm engulfed in their show and learn lessons with every episode. For example, Kim Kardashian appeared in promotional ads for the launch of her makeup line, KKW Beauty. One of the photos was lit in such a way that people accused her of blackface. The press and social media went crazy and Kim was shocked and upset. She took the ads down immediately and was nervous about the public outcry. I don't think she needed to cave in that situation. Clearly it wasn't her intention to do blackface, and the photo doesn't even look like it. She said she was really tan at the time and that it was just the way the images were tweaked. But she was so worried about offending people that she took them down.

Did she really feel like the ad wasn't tasteful, or was she just pleasing her audience? We will never know, but she does.

In another episode, her sister Kendall Jenner gets major backlash for appearing in a Pepsi commercial where she's seen joining a protest and then giving a Pepsi to a police officer. Social media attacked her for being insensitive to the Black Lives Matter movement. As a kind, thoughtful person, she was devastated. She kept saying, "I should never have been part of it." But I don't agree. Again, like Kim, Kendall was well-intentioned. She needs to look in the mirror and say, "Did I do this to hurt people? No. Have I explained that I didn't do this to hurt people? Yes." So then why do you need to back into a hole and beat yourself up? Why should you apologize if you're not wrong?

This brings me to my second point: always apologize when you *are* wrong. This is equally important, because sometimes we say things we shouldn't. Sometimes you get overly passionate, but instead of digging deeper on things you're wrong about, say you're wrong. Plain and simple. Sometimes, for example, we watch the response to the State of the Union address and get fired up and say inappropriate things about Joe Kennedy on Instagram. I did that, and it was wrong. I scrutinized myself and beat myself up. *Why did you do that? That was so stupid*, I thought. *You could have lost your job.* But I learned from it. And at some point, when you learn your lesson, you can't keep browbeating yourself. That won't get you anywhere. So I owned up to it and apologized for the mistake.

When you own your shit, you reach a different level. It's also really healing to recognize your poison and when you are standing in your way. So when you make a mistake with a partner, parent, employer, friend, or whomever, admit it and move on. It's that simple. When you hurt someone's feelings, you are rude to someone, or you overreact, just apologize if you truly mean it. It's much easier than being defensive or dodging what you've done. If the other person chooses *not* to accept your apology, that's on them. Regardless, it's going to change your life because people will respect the fact that you understand you've made a mistake. And this will make you even more powerful when you are right.

The truth is this: you are magic—with or without "likes." So "like" yourself, believe that you are magic, and have the confidence to know that no one can touch your magical ass!

Chapter 6

BE A VOICE FOR
THE VOICELESS.

When we speak, we are our afraid our words will not
be heard or welcomed. But when we are silent, we are
still afraid. So it is better to speak.
—AUDRE LORDE

In April 2018, on-duty police officer Rogelio Santander,
twenty-seven, died the day after he was shot during an
attempted arrest at a Home Depot in Dallas. His partner, Officer Crystal Almeida, twenty-six, was shot in the
face and Scott Painter, a Home Depot loss prevention officer, was shot three times during the attack, in his head
and one shoulder. Both were critically wounded. As the

two police officers were trying to detain a shoplifting suspect, he pulled out a gun. Almeida has had several surgeries to remove bullet fragments and excess fluid from her brain and facial reconstruction. She also lost sight in her left eye. But if you haven't heard about this, you're not alone. That story was nowhere to be found. Why? Because instead of focusing on this *real* news, the media focused on the fact that Kanye West tweeted his support for Trump that same week. Yes, Kanye seemed to be all that everyone was talking about on TV, Twitter, and Instagram. To me, this intense coverage of a nut-job celebrity and all the people hopping on the Kanye band-wagon was absurd. More important, it really hit home because my best friend, Laura, is a police officer who was supposed to be on duty at that Home Depot! She wound up working the NFL Draft instead, but she easily could have been in the line of fire that day. And *that* is why I do what I do and why I will continue to be a voice for the voiceless, in this case the officers who died that day working at the Home Depot and every officer, first responder, member of the United States military, and American who risks his or her life for something bigger. I know that I'm blessed with the platform that I have and I'm going to use it to uplift these heroes, people who in-spire me. Something I often say when I give speeches to law enforcement or the military is "I know a lot of you are excited that I'm here for you tonight, but I'm just a girl from South Dakota with a big mouth, and I'm going to use it to fight for *you*."

Although a lot of people criticize me, many, many people tell me they admire me for being brave. But that's a tricky word. I'm not brave. I'm bold because I say what's on my mind, whether it's politically correct or not. Those officers at Home Depot were brave. The people who fight for this country are brave. Originally the title of this book was "Brave Enough to Say It." But upon reflection, that adjective is incorrect, and it's something I'm really sensitive to. Brave is people who die for this country and the loved ones who make sacrifices that go along with that. Brave is the police officers who pull over cars and are not sure if they're going to get shot or not. Brave is knocking on the door for a domestic violence call and possibly getting jumped, stabbed, or shot in the process. That's brave.

Bravery is not celebrities on either side of the political aisle speaking their minds. An activist tweeted that Kanye "is the bravest man in America" because he went on *Saturday Night Live* and said his "Make America Great Again" hat was his superhero cape. The activist said he was a "hero." Are you kidding me? This was even more infuriating because it was on the one-year anniversary of the shooting in Las Vegas where fifty-eight people were gunned down and first responders and police officers rushed toward danger to protect their fellow Americans. People in the crowd were reaching out to and caring for total strangers in the midst of that dangerous chaos. Now *that* is brave. Kanye? No. Note to Kanye worshippers: if incoherent celebrity endorsements mattered, Hillary Clinton would be your president.

People in law enforcement and the military are the definition of brave, but sadly, they are often voiceless because they can't speak up for themselves or their fellow officers or service members while they are on active duty. Can you imagine that? All this stuff is going on around them that can threaten their lives, that directly impacts them, and they are not allowed to say anything? They are advised not to talk about politics or race issues or anything else. So I want to say the things they're thinking, and I'm not *guessing* what these things are. I spend time with them. I *talk* to them. I ask about their thoughts and worries, their fears and frustrations. I talk to family members who have had their loved ones killed in the line of duty.

Law enforcement officers have a special place in my heart, and they always will. That's why I push back so fiercely on those who denigrate and demonize them. The story of police officer Corporal Ronil Singh from Newman, California, is just one example.

"Looks like he got a gunshot wound to the head."

That was the call heard over the police scanner around 1 a.m. after Corporal Singh was shot and killed during a traffic stop when the suspect pulled a gun on him. This was shortly after Christmas. Oh, and did I mention that the suspect was a man who is, yes, in this country *illegally.* Corporal Singh was just thirty-three years old. He was working additional overtime after already working Christmas Day to make extra money to support his wife and five-month-old son. Unlike his killer, Corporal Singh came to this country *legally,* from Fiji.

Imagine being Mrs. Singh and taking a Christmas photo with your infant son and husband, then watching him leave for work not knowing it was the last photo you would take as a family, not knowing it would be the last Christmas you'd ever spend with him. That's the gut-wrenching true story Mrs. Singh will have to tell their son one day, the gut-wrenching story her son will have to live with, and the same gut-wrenching story so many law enforcement families must tell. It takes a special kind of person to put on a badge and uniform for little money, horrible hours, and what seems like little respect. It also takes a special kind of family to sit back and watch their loved one put on that uniform and badge and walk out the door, the family not knowing if he or she will come home.

Corporal Singh was shot during a traffic stop. Think about that: you're an officer, walking up to a car not knowing what or who you'll find. People call this a "routine" traffic stop, but *nothing* is routine when you are a police officer. Those who hold that thin blue line put their lives at risk *every* second of *every* shift. And they do it for *us*. They do it so we can spend Christmas nights with our families. They do it so we can watch our five-month-old children grow up. So people like Nancy Pelosi and Chuck Schumer can defend illegal immigrants and sanctuary cities.

We can't bring back Corporal Ronil Singh. He paid the ultimate price and made the ultimate sacrifice and no amount of "thoughts and prayers" will ever turn back time on this awful story. Yet what I *can* do is use my platform to honor his memory. I bet you know these names: Alton Sterling, Freddie Gray, Michael Brown, and Sandra Bland. But think about it: do you know the name of even one officer we lost this year? You may know that Miley Cyrus finally married her on-again, off-again boyfriend or that Kim Kardashian brought real snow in for her Los Angeles Christmas party, but do you pay attention, retweet, or share when you hear "end of watch"? We need to change that. We need to make sure men like Corporal Singh are not just mourned for a day on the local news, but rather remembered for years and years to come. That is my mission and I will never stop defending those who protect and defend me and you.

About a year and a half ago, I had the incredible honor of attending an event for the Concerns of Police Survivors (COPS), an organization of family members who have lost loved ones in the line of duty. I spoke at their Black & Blue Ball to a sold-out crowd of people, pouring out my love for law enforcement. After the speech, I took pictures with them for four and a half hours—865 professional photos and hundreds of selfies. A group of women came up to me toward the end.

"Thank you for staying all this time to take pictures," one of them said to me. "You must be so tired." Am I tired? Yes. But are they going to see that? No. Absolutely not. The people at that event were there because they lost husbands, wives, fathers, mothers, daughters, or sons who were protecting *our* communities. Their loved ones get up and put on a uniform every day and do work that's much harder than mine. So if I can give them a picture or two or three and talk to them for a little while and that's somehow going to give them some joy, I'll stand there for ten hours with a smile on my face and never act like I'm too good for that.

I'm going to take a picture with everyone who wants one because they're going to walk away and say, "Tomi stayed. She talks it, and she walks it." Nothing is more disheartening to me than when I see people who have become too big for their britches, and they're too good for other people, especially the people who support their careers and causes. I remember being with Glenn Beck at events and after his speech, he'd take a few pictures, shake a few hands, and leave after fifteen minutes. Even at his *own* charity events. I would never walk into any room, whether it was a doctor's office waiting room, the set of a show I'm on, or anywhere else and treat people poorly. People remember that. The kind of person that I aspire to be is someone who can turn around, and the people I worked with at Express or One America, even at *The Blaze,* have only kind words to say about me, about how I treat people and about my work ethic. I remember watching Glenn leave his own events and thinking to myself, I will never be like that. I will never bring all these people here who are excited to see me and just leave. After all, it's the people who come to those events who keep me going every day.

I can walk away from that event with law enforcement exhausted and losing my voice because it's the least I can do.

Some of the people I took pictures with were widows whose husbands were killed in the line of duty. Some were *my* age and recently married or pregnant. But now they'd lost their husbands and were left to raise those children alone. They told me, "We love what you do, and we're so thankful. Thanks for being our voice."

One of the pictures I took at the Black & Blue Ball was with Officer Kirk Griess, a Marine Corps veteran, and his wife. Nine months later, the president of COPS wrote to tell me that Officer Griess was struck and killed during a traffic stop on Interstate 80, leaving his wife and young children behind. Now that he was deceased, his wife had asked if I could sign the picture I took with them that night, because it meant so much to their family.

That gave me chills. It's important to speak the truth and speak it loudly. It's essential to speak it loudly when it's on behalf of someone else.

This wonderful man died in the line of duty. I was so honored to meet him and his wife. I don't do all this because I like trending on Twitter. Who the hell cares about that when I got to give a message of love and hope and appreciation to this officer and his family? I will always be a voice for law enforcement. They give and sacrifice so much for the rest of us. Mothers, fathers, brothers, sisters, husbands, wives, and all Americans send our warriors into the line of duty in our country and overseas to protect and defend our freedom. They don't ask for much in return, so they should never be abandoned overseas or here at home. This is not a Republican issue. This is not a Democratic issue. This an issue of basic, human decency for people who selflessly put their lives on the line to protect us every day.

However, the voiceless are not just police officers and
the military. They also include everyday, hardworking,
blue-collar Americans. Contrary to popular belief, Make
America Great Again is not about a conservative resurgence. It's about a hardworking, God-fearing resurgence
of the American people. Over the past thirty years, we've
seen a war against middle America waged by the coastal
elite. It's not a Republican-versus-Democrats thing. Leaders of both parties spent all their time in cities and lost
sight of what the rest of us were up to.

For decades, the American worker has been drop-
kicked by both political parties. But it hasn't just been
those steel, coal, and factory workers. American farmers
and cattlemen have also been kicked in the teeth. I know.
My uncle is a rancher and feels the pinch every day. Yet
you don't hear much about that. Why? Because the flyover
states don't matter to the mainstream media. Well, I'm going to use my voice, my platform—and your attention—to
change that. Imagine your entire livelihood dictated by
the bank, the weather, and luck. Yeah. American cowboys
and cattlemen have never had it easy. But these last few
years have been brutal. The costs of raising U.S. cattle have
risen, while the price earned on that cattle has dropped.
Many ranchers struggle to stay operational. It's a daily battle and one you'll hardly hear them complain about. They
don't want a government handout—just a fighting chance.

This is why I've been on a crusade fighting tirelessly for country-of-origin labeling for beef products. This is close to my heart because I come from a ranching family, but it's an issue no one talks about because it's not a sex scandal, it's not a war, and it's not a terrorist attack. It's not a border wall or any other issue that grabs the headlines. Even the Trump administration won't listen to these ranchers, and the secretary of agriculture brushes them off. I fight to get it on the news, and they shut me out. Even my network is reluctant to give it the attention it deserves. I get it, it's not flashy—*but* it *is* important! People don't know where their meat is coming from and to me that's a bipartisan issue.

Under regulations Trump inherited from the Obama administration, the beef you find in a local grocery store can be labeled "Product of USA" as long as it was packaged here. So it could have been born, raised, and slaughtered virtually anywhere. Let's say half a carcass of beef arrives from Uruguay. A U.S. packer can cut that carcass up in a U.S. packing plant and label it "Product of USA." Even worse? If a packer unwraps that meat and simply rewraps it, it can be labeled "Product of USA." So when I say I want to be a voice for the voiceless, this is what I mean. There's an entire organization of independent cattle farmers (R-CALF) whose membership had dwindled to less than 100 members from 2,500 at its height. But then

I gave a speech at their convention and have been talking about this issue since I was at One America. I've talked about it on *The Blaze*, my Facebook page, Fox News, and in "Final Thoughts," and since then their membership has ballooned to an all-time high. And I won't stop talking about it until we get country-of-origin labeling and give our American ranchers what they deserve.

When I express my thoughts, it's not about me. It's not about fame. It's not to get celebrities to talk about me. It's to use my platform to talk about real things and real people. I don't need to give Kanye a voice; he's got a voice. I don't need to reinforce his message. I need to reinforce the voice of the voiceless, and that spans so many people. It's more than the military and law enforcement. It's people in middle America, people living alongside farmers and ranchers and coal miners. It's people like Tammy Crabtree. The summer of my junior year of college at UNLV, I was in a women's studies class called Race, Gender, and Class. Yeah, I know what you're thinking: why would I take a class like that? Was I just setting myself up for high blood pressure? No. I strive to keep an open mind even when it's uncomfortable. Most of the class was bogus and *did* make my blood boil—after all, it was a daily feeding of identity politics and the victimhood narrative, which by now you know I *hate*! However, there was one section about social class that will always stick with me. We watched the PBS documentary *People Like Us*, featuring this woman Tammy Crabtree. Tammy lived with her teenage sons in a beat-up old trailer in a run-down trailer park. She gladly welcomed the camera crew into her humble home. She didn't seem the least bit embarrassed, but her sons certainly were. They told the film crew they were ashamed of their trailer, their lifestyle, and the way their mom dressed. She would always wear her Burger King uniform, likely because it was about all she had.

Tammy worked at Burger King cleaning the bathrooms. She didn't have a car, so she walked several miles to and from work each day. On her trek, people driving by her would yell nasty comments like "Trashy bitch," among others. Yet she kept going undeterred. The producers asked Tammy why she kept working at Burger King when it would be much easier for her to just get on welfare and food stamps.

"Why would I be on welfare when I can work?" she said, clearly insulted by the suggestion. Her story touched me for many reasons. Here was a woman who was not only a single mother raising teenage sons in a beat-up trailer, but also a woman who didn't complain about it. She is the average American, but like most average Americans, she is exceptional. I don't know what ever happened to Tammy Crabtree and her family but I think about her often. She is the kind of person who inspires me.

When I talk about the voiceless, I'm also talking about young girls in college who don't have the confidence to say what they think and Republicans who have moved to cities but don't drink the liberal Kool-Aid. It's the families of innocent people killed by criminal illegal aliens and anyone who lost their job to someone overseas. I also mean people who don't feel confident like Kim, the woman who came up to me at a restaurant and told me that she was in her forties before she ever stood up for herself.

If I have to get a little aggressive, heated, and passionate to get their side out there, then that's what's going to happen, because they need to be heard. When one side has been bullied into silence, I feel like I have to break through that, because I'm not going to sit back. And I'm also not going to let people intimidate me into shutting up.

Last year I was walking alone at night in New York City.

"Tomi, I'm such a fan. Can I get a picture with you?" asked a guy in his twenties.

"Sure," I said. When I leaned in for the selfie, he was videoing and said, "How does it feel to be a racist piece of shit?" Another time I was in Hermosa Beach, California, with my friends. I was walking to the bathroom alone when this girl about my age grabbed my shoulder.

"Are you Tomi?"

"Yes, I am. Nice to meet you," I said as I reached out my hand.

"You're a piece of shit, and you're not welcome in my town!" she yelled. I was furious, so I had to sit there and take what I call "a fiver." This is when I pause and take five seconds to think about how I'm going to react, because in this case I could have gone off on the girl or I could just walk away. I grabbed *her* shoulder and I said, "I don't think that you get to decide that, but I hope you have a good night."

These things upset me, but I'm still going to treat every person who comes up to me with respect. If they're going to be horrible, that says more about *their* character than mine, and I'm not going to stop taking pictures and being friendly just because some people want to exploit me. It's not always easy, and I do get angry. But every time I feel that way and when I just want to get out my revenge, I pray to God to please keep my intentions pure. Then I take a step back and realize that this is not about Glenn Beck, *The Blaze*, or some rude stranger at a bar. I can't control those people; I can only control my reaction. Some people are going to wrong you no matter how well you treat them. But don't let that embitter you. Don't let *their* bad behavior change the way *you* act.

People will say, "Did you see what so-and-so said about you?" and I'll shake my head. Don't read the filth. Don't let it bring you down. Don't put a lot of thought into someone you think very little of. If that's not a person you want to spend your time with, don't spend your time *on* them. Period. Why would I acknowledge these haters by reading their comments? Why would I sulk and say "poor me"? My time is too valuable. I want to be a voice for the voiceless, not a voice for the assholes. I've got things to do. And so do you! You're not going to get me angry because I've seen it all and been through it all. It's just white noise to me. The truth is, if you don't like me and still watch everything I do, you are a fan. I also know that every time someone attacks me, he or she is projecting his or her insecurity on me. They're trying to find holes in *me* to make themselves feel better. Good luck with that!

Recently I had two incidents within a day of each other that were telling. The first was at a restaurant in Manhattan Beach, California. Come to think of it, this organic, vegan place isn't where I'm going to find a lot of friends, but my boyfriend and I were grabbing dinner before a movie. A young woman in her twenties who appeared to be the manager was walking toward the back of the restaurant when she stopped and saw me.

"Hey, Tomi," she said.

"Nice to meet you," I said, reaching out my hand as I always do in these situations. "What's your name?"

"I think you live in the wrong city," she said in a bitchy tone. And this was the *manager* of a restaurant. Could you imagine? I'd like to think that if Nancy Pelosi or Lena Dunham were eating at [name a place to eat in your town growing up], the people there would have the common Christian decency to be polite.

The next night, I was at a bar when a girl came up to me and said, "Are you Tomi?"

"Yes," I said, feeling a little wary from the day before.

"I appreciate everything that you do," she said. "It's so hard for women to be outspoken and I've really struggled with it. But watching you has slowly brought me out of my shell. You've really helped me in my life." So, I had that bitchy manager the day before and this girl the next. Which one was I going to give weight to? Someone who just wanted to be nasty? Or a girl who was one of the voiceless but is finding her way and looks to me as an inspiration? It's not that one was a supporter or a conservative and the other wasn't. It's that one girl just wanted to tell me something mean, and the other wanted to tell me something that helped her. Situations like that make me realize and recalibrate my purpose.

I will never let people harden me, and I will never stop

doing my job because people say mean things. I don't do what I do for the asshole who comes up to me in the street and calls me a piece of shit. I do this for the fifteen-year-old girls and their mothers who tell me I'm their role model and that I've inspired them to stand up for themselves. I do it for the police officers, the firefighters, the soldiers, the service members, and their family members who have lost loved ones. I do it for the people in middle America who don't have a voice, for the average American working person who is just trying to get by and doesn't want anything from anyone, but is getting kicked around. I'm not going to stop being a voice for these people because someone is going to comment on Twitter, Instagram, or in person. So if I have to be the shield in front of them, that's fine. I have rhino skin.

Chapter 7

BEFORE YOU ASK YOURSELF WHY SOME PEOPLE HATE YOU, ASK YOURSELF WHY YOU GIVE A DAMN.

Worry less about who you might offend and pay
more attention to who you might inspire.

In July 2018, during a press conference with Vladimir Putin, President Trump said, "I don't see any reason why it would be" Russia that meddled in the 2016 election. A day later he clarified that remark, saying he misspoke and insisting that he *did* accept evidence showing that Russia did in fact meddle. He added that he had the utmost respect for our intelligence agencies. I took the president at his word, but his critics wouldn't let it go. After his initial remarks, a few people actually accused him of committing treason! Despite what the left would have you believe, there was no evidence Russian meddling had any impact on the election outcome. Still, many people in the press and the left were outraged and criticized him about it, but I didn't agree and said so when I appeared on *Fox & Friends*. "I'm fed up. . . . These are the final stages of Trump Derangement Syndrome, and you're going to see it more and more as we head into the midterms, but I'll have folks look at this and ask the Democrats, many of the Never Trumpers and many in the mainstream media, 'Do you want this president to wage war against Russia because Hillary Clinton lost the election?'" Clearly Trump was watching because minutes later he tweeted this: "Some people HATE the fact that I got along well with President Putin of Russia. They would rather go to war than see this. It's called Trump Derangement Syndrome." The media and public went nuts commenting on what they said was Trump parroting my words. Someone said, "This is why Mattel never made Barbie talk." But comments like that don't bother me. To me, it's hilarious, and I turn it around. Barbie is a multibillion-dollar industry so call me Barbie all you want! But I don't always feel this way. In the last couple of weeks, I got raked over the coals by conservatives because of my abortion stance. Because

I didn't agree with *their* stance on abortion. Nasty things were said and I was attacked not just for my beliefs but as a person. They were diminishing me as a conservative, trying to downgrade my intelligence, reducing me to just a pretty girl who goes on TV and talks.

Just because I have a tough exterior doesn't mean that these personal attacks don't get to me, because they absolutely do. I have feelings, too. And that's when I have to take a step back and remember who I am and why I do this. I also had to sit down and analyze what it was that upset me. It didn't bother me that they were questioning my beliefs. I'm fine when people do that. What bothered me was the essence of all these articles and tweets was that I'm dumb and the only reason I am where I am is that I'm pretty. They were so quick to reduce me and call me stupid just because my belief didn't match up with theirs. And yes, that hurt my feelings. (It's also the root of what is wrong with politics today. Conservatives bitch that the left is unloving and intolerant but then attack someone when he or she doesn't agree with them on an issue.)

I always try to take a step back and evaluate my feelings. In this instance, I had to examine why I was feeling crappy about certain people calling me names. Otherwise, it would eat at me. I traced it back and had this little dialogue with myself:

What's bothering you? What is it that's getting at you? Is it because people disagree with you?

No, that's not it.

Is it because people are challenging your point of view?

No. that's not it.

And then it hit me: it's because people were saying I'm dumb. So I investigated that, asking myself, Why does it bother me that Erick Erickson and Ben Shapiro think I'm dumb? Why do I have a real sensitivity to that word? Well, likely because I've worked hard to get where I am and I've had men throughout my life telling me I'm just dumb. Boyfriends, bosses, and randoms. That was it. It's a trigger point for me that goes back to my first boyfriend, Brian, who was verbally abusive and condescending. We started dating in our sophomore year of high school and went to UNLV together. He got a baseball scholarship and saw himself as a big deal. I was going to be a journalist, but he would tell me I wasn't going to amount to anything. "What are you going to do? Be a reporter in a Podunk town in Iowa making twenty thousand dollars a year?" He would belittle me and belittle my dreams. He also cheated on me many times. After two years, he broke up with me in the parking lot of a fast-food restaurant. And yet I kept getting back together with him.

Mr. H, my boss at One America, was another one of

those men in my life. One day I was in his office, where I thought we were having a friendly conversation.

"I think all women are stupid," he said. I thought he was kidding.

"You're laughing like you think I'm joking," he said, putting his feet up on the desk next to his full security setup. He had cameras everywhere so he could watch what his employees were doing.

"Do you think *I'm* stupid?" I asked.

"Well, you're a woman, ain't you? But you think like a man, so I don't know. Kind of halfway." I was offended, but what could I do? There was no HR department and even if there was, I wouldn't have reported him. You may say, "Why would you work for someone who says women are stupid?" First of all, I *know* I'm not stupid. Second, for me to quit because of that and miss out on the opportunity to have my own show wasn't going to hurt *him,* it was going to hurt me. I'd rather say, "You think women are stupid? I'll show you that they're not." I'd rather have someone tell me that I'm less-than and prove that I'm more-than. It would be nice if we lived in this idealistic world where that isn't the case, but we don't. So I had a choice: I could either sit in the corner and cry or I could get to work. Victim isn't a cute look. It's not fun. It's not empowering. It just brings you down.

Even if you don't consider yourself a feminist or don't

associate with that movement, you may still experience challenges or have additional obstacles like these because you're a woman. But I'm not going to say I'm a victim because of it and I'm not going to cause a big scene about it and get people in trouble. Yes, I was in this position experiencing something that men in my field don't experience as much, but I'm not going to let that limit me. When situations like that arise, you have a choice in terms of how you react because you are responsible for your actions and reactions. You may feel like you've been victimized, discriminated against, written off, or put in a box. You may feel like you have limitations put on you for any number of reasons. Maybe it's because of your gender, your skin color, your upbringing, the way you talk, where you live, or what field you went into. That doesn't mean you should sit there and write a sob story.

This brings me to the reason why I'm frustrated with the feminist movement and why I don't consider myself a feminist: this movement used to be for all women, like an umbrella we could all live under. It was about female empowerment, which I believe in. I love to be inspired by strong women and to inspire other women. However, that was hijacked by modern-day feminists who are wearing pussy hats and screaming at men in the streets. They're protesting to get attention. I don't think that's empowering anybody. How is that helping the girl who is in her first job and is discriminated against because she is a woman? When she looks at women in the streets screaming with hats on, does that empower her? Does that make her part of a movement? I don't think so, and I think that's a disservice to all women. Female empowerment is wanting your fellow women to break through barriers. It's wanting them not to feel limited and not to feel like victims.

However, I think that modern-day feminism is *all* about telling women they are victims and what you can get out of it. Just twenty years ago, feminism used to be about equality. Now it's about special treatment, and I don't think we should get special treatment. The fact that we've gotten to a point where feminism is about wearing pussy hats and how big a payout you can get is disgusting to me. Find your voice, not your pussy hats! Yes, maybe I get paid less than men doing the same job as me. And yes, it drives me crazy. But I'm going to keep working my ass off and one day I'll be able to call my own shots. That's going to be the best revenge, *not* begging for special treatment.

People say, "You're against feminists, but you wouldn't be where you are today if it weren't for them." Yes, I acknowledge the work that classic feminists have done for me and my career and I will never discount that. When Geraldine Ferraro became the first female Democrat vice presidential candidate, women everywhere celebrated.

When Sarah Palin became the first female Republican vice presidential candidate, feminists said, "Sorry, not that kind of woman."

Modern-day #feminists have ruined all that work to attain equality, to get rights, to empower themselves. They've thrown that in the trash because they hate Donald Trump. They have also characterized him as what masculinity is, so they are not only in a crusade against Trump, they are in a crusade against masculinity, and that's damaging. That's why it's important for me to address feminism and take this issue head-on.

Now they're interested in attacking other women, tearing down men, telling white women to shut up, and using victimhood as an excuse for their failings. Although this is not a book just for conservative women, I have to acknowledge the conservative women who feel like they have no place to go. Conservative women have been cast out by the feminist movement, and that's not just *me* saying it. It's the leaders of the progressive feminist movement actively saying, "You are not one of us. You are not part of the women's movement." That's Congresswoman Maxine Waters telling her supporters to publicly confront the Trump administration about the separation of families at the border and Michelle Wolf making fun of Sarah Huckabee Sanders at the White House Correspondents' Association Dinner. That's Kathy Griffin calling Sanders the new linebacker for the Dallas Cowboys. That's Linda Sarsour, cochair of the Women's March (and also a vocal supporter of sharia law), protesting against Donald Trump and saying that women like journalist Brigitte Gabriel and human rights activist Ayaan Hirsi Ali should have their vaginas confiscated because they are conservatives and because they speak out against Sarsour's selective brand of feminism.

I look up to women of all political affiliations but let's be honest, conservative women aren't nearly as celebrated, and are indeed a million times more denigrated than any liberal. It's okay to humiliate and harass women, so long as they are conservative or have the last name Trump. Where were the feminists when rapper Bow Wow threatened to "pimp out" the first lady? Or what about self-proclaimed feminist Chelsea Handler, who said she wouldn't have Melania Trump on her show because she can barely speak English? Let's not forget the mainstream media coverage of Melania's shoe choice after Hurricane Harvey, the shoes considered breaking news.

Where were the feminists when a *Daily Beast* writer referred to Sarah Huckabee Sanders as a butch queen? Or the nonstop, personal attacks on Kellyanne Conway? Or what about the leftist-led boycott and removal of Ivanka Trump's clothing line from several major retailers? If these women were on the left they'd be on the cover of

Vogue; they'd be celebrated and given a gold feminist star. It seems to me like the leftist mainstream media and the feminist warriors are often the real bullies and, above all else, major hypocrites. Yeah, they are all about preaching tolerance, acceptance, and female empowerment—but only for some, only if you're the kind of woman they like.

This goes back to mean girls and bringing other women down, and to me *that* is a flaw that the feminist movement has not addressed. They have addressed the political element of wanting free birth control and abortion rights, but they haven't addressed the real thing that holds women back, which, in my opinion, is other women. During the 2016 election, former secretary of state Madeleine Albright came out and said, "There's a special place in hell for women who don't support other women." Obviously she was referring to those who didn't support Hillary. What I want to make very clear is that when you support other women, it's not about rubber-stamping *all* women just *because* we have the same biological makeup. I think that's wrong. Women are not victims. So if someone wants our votes, they're going to have to appeal to our brains, hearts, and pocketbooks, not just what's between our legs.

During hearings for Supreme Court nominee Brett Kavanaugh, a lot of women said we should believe his accuser just because she was a woman. Why? Women are just as capable of lying and scheming as anyone else. (Look at Hillary Clinton!) You can't take every word they say as gospel. That's infuriating to me as a woman. It's not about supporting them no matter what they're doing. No. It's about supporting them when they're doing good things, when they're achieving and they're successful doing it the right way, and they're authentic. It's also being able to call out other women when they're doing something wrong. It's not a rubber stamp, but it's also not tearing down other women when they're successful because you feel threatened, diminished, or jealous of them.

I support other women all day long who have done great things for other women. I have incredible respect for Oprah Winfrey even though I don't like her politics and a lot of the things she's done and advocated for. But I respect the hell out of her. Being a conservative means learning to respect and admire people you disagree with. Most liberals have no idea, especially big-city liberals.

Another example is Chelsea Handler. As I said earlier, I grew up watching her, and later I had the opportunity to meet and debate her onstage. As a result, I've always respected what she's been able to do in a man's world. She has never said, "There are no other women who are late-night talk show hosts, and I'm a woman so I should replace Jay Leno." She never said she should be the token woman in her field. Instead she said, "I'm going to do what I'm going to do because I'm the best at it." Period. I respect her immensely for that, even though I find some of the things she does and says to be atrocious. Chelsea is on that feminist bandwagon. She's got her pussy hat on and led the post-inauguration Women's March in Park City, Utah, at the Sundance Film Festival. Yet, throughout her impressive career, not once did she ever say, "Poor me," or say that she should have something in her career because she's a woman. I wonder if she realizes that. If she did, I think she'd get off the feminist bandwagon.

I'm sickened and disgusted by the way the current generation of feminists have hijacked the movement and turned it into something it was not intended to be. You have your Tumblr posters and pussy hat knitters, and then you have the women who are going out and being successful. They are the women who are working hard to become good at their jobs, whether they're working to be CEO or are going to be a firefighter or police officer. I don't look at someone like Lena Dunham as a role model among women. In her book, she described a creepy incident where she looked inside her little sister's vagina. There was also controversy about the identity of her college rapist. Her television show probably set gender equality back ten years. It eventually came under attack from all the social justice warriors she set out to impress.

Instead, I look at my friend Laura, who is a police

officer and works on crimes against children. She busts
pedophiles every single day. Or I look at the new chief
of United States Border Patrol, Carla Provost. She's
achieved the highest level of success in what used to be a
man's world. She gets it done and doesn't cry about it. Yet
where are the feminists cheering for her? Where is her
Cosmo magazine cover?

When I went on a border tour, I asked some of the female border patrol officers what it was like to be a woman
on that force. They said they were really sick of hearing that
question, because they don't get up every day and think,
I'm a woman. They don't get up in the morning and check
their ovaries. My point is that if you constantly think you're
a woman in a man's world, you're not going to get very far.
I don't believe there is one woman who is successful who
wakes up and says she is going to do or not do something
because she's a woman. When you focus on your gender,
race, economic status, or social class, that's a limitation.
It's not that those things don't exist, but if you let them dictate *your* life and put you in some kind of box, you're never
going to achieve anything. The most successful, empowering women are out there accomplishing things, not talking
about what they're not getting. Don't let your results be a
product of your lame excuses. You're better than that.

Imagine if, as a culture, we taught personal responsibility, not victimhood. Imagine how much you'd propel

yourself if *that* were your focus. A few months ago, I was at a Starbucks in Washington, D.C., with my producer. We were sitting at a table and near us waiting in line was an older white woman and in front of her a younger black girl. All of a sudden, they got into a big altercation because one of them got the last spinach egg wrap. (You can't make this stuff up!) They were both yelling horrible things at each other when the black girl turned around and said, "You and your white privilege." *What?* Was she seriously pulling out white privilege, racism, and the civil rights movement over a spinach wrap? Was this girl playing the victim over breakfast? Yes, there are situations you can't get yourself out of, but if you *can* get yourself out of a situation and you choose not to, that's on you. Why be a victim when you can be a warrior?

Let's take the water-throwing incident in Minnesota as an example. After the girl threw water at me, I didn't want to create a big scene and I really just wanted to leave. The funny thing about this situation is that I would never have talked about it publicly if *they* hadn't. I wasn't going to discuss it. I'm not a victim. I'd never go out and say, "Look what happened to me." I knew it was just girls showing off and trying to be nasty. Don't get me wrong; it was upsetting. I was trying to have brunch with my parents. However, it didn't affect me long-term. I don't remember their faces. Sadly, that incident will likely be the highlight of their lives. It will truly be their fifteen minutes of fame. Well, not mine. I'm not scarred by it. I'm not going to sit here and say I'm traumatized. I'm just going to learn from it. Because if you can learn and reflect on an experience or situation, then you're not a victim of it any longer. Then you can move on. It was a shitty thing they did to me, but at the end of the day, I don't cry over spilled milk or tossed water.

That's what happened with the *Roe v. Wade* controversy. Once I identified and isolated it, I thought, *Okay. So today am I going to worry that* Ben Shapiro *said I'm not as smart as he is?*

No. It's another man telling me what I am, how intelligent I am allowed to seem, and trying to measure his fantasy version of me by *his* barometer of acceptance.

At some level, everybody cares what people think about them. To me it's about prioritizing how you feel about yourself. That's what I do now. So-and-so doesn't like me? I take a pause and ask myself, *Do I really care?* If my mom is mad at me and doesn't like something I did, yes, I care. A lot. I know she and I are on the same team and want what's best for each other. When I do something to my boyfriend, and he's upset with me, I care.

Your close friends, family, and loved ones love you, care about you, and have the best intentions, so, yes, if you've upset or hurt them, it matters. But worrying about what anyone else thinks, especially mean girls or strangers on social media, will drain your energy. Think about what someone else's motives are. Most people who insult you never thought for a second about how you would feel, having only thought about how the insult would make *them* feel. If I worried what people thought during the Glenn Beck lawsuit, when conservatives raked me over the coals, or when people on social media say that I'm ugly or they hate me, that would drain my time and energy. If I had let that happen, I would not be where I am or be able to do what I do today. It's knowing what to give your energy to and not to.

I want my energy to go to the people who listen when I say we can do better together, not the people who want to see me doing worse.

You don't have to be in the public eye to have to deal with this. I would encourage you to try to analyze your feelings, too. Let's say you have a girl in school who is a little bitch. Let's call her Katie. And Katie is going around telling everyone that you're a slut or dumb or ugly and other people agree with her. Even though it's not true, of course it gets to you. That's okay. You're human. You have feelings. But I want you to stop and think about it. Take a moment and ask yourself, What is it in Katie's life that makes her so unhappy she needs to diminish and reduce you? Because she's insecure about something. Let's say you have a Senate minority leader who is a little bitch. Same thing.

It's funny to me because I've got grown, middle-aged men who run businesses and who went to Harvard coming at me on Twitter with ad hominem attacks because they are so insecure. Instead of challenging me on my beliefs, they're challenging me on their understanding of my intelligence and passing me off as some "pretty girl who says things." Ha. That's what you think.

When people tell me I'm dumb or that I just got where I am professionally because of my appearance or that I'm not a real conservative, I have to bring it back to real life.

Their real problem is that they have an idea of what a conservative has to look like—old, male, technologically inept, out of step with pop culture—and I'm the opposite of this. They don't want someone who looks like me advocating old-fashioned values, because it ruins the liberal narrative.

I always ask myself, "Tomi, do you believe what you're saying? Is it rooted in something? Can you stand behind it?"

Yes. It always is. Yes, I always do.

"So, if that's true, why do you care that these people don't respect you?" People hate me for who they *think* I am—a robot, racist, a mean girl, you name it—not for who I am. They don't *want* to get to know me. Why? Because they don't want to change their misperceptions. It's easier to paint someone as a monster than to take time to get to know them. Making me the enemy of humanity validates their worldview and allows them to write me off. They don't want to think of me as a human being with a heart and soul and feelings. If they did, they would have to get to know me and that takes effort. They don't want to put in that effort. It's easier to label me as an evil bitch and leave it at that.

For example, Kathy Griffin, a well-known Trump critic, has sparred with me numerous times on social media. Although I disagree with almost everything she says, tweets, or does, including posting herself holding Donald Trump's decapitated head, I still want to sit down and have a conversation with her. I know that behind all the craziness and anger is a human being and I want to get to know her and vice versa. But when I invited her to do an interview with me at Fox Nation, not only did she refuse, but she tweeted the email from Fox News and wrote, "Fuck you." It's laziness to exist in your bubble and play to your team. Being called a Nazi is not fun. Hearing people say I hate black people is not fun (or true). But it's not reality, so why let anyone with their toxic energy disrupt my peace and tranquility? And why waste your time trying to disprove people who are dead set on misunderstanding you?

As a political commentator it's my job to talk about politics. As a human being, it's my job to put people over politics. Kathy and I go round and round on social media on dang near a weekly basis but that doesn't matter to me. Her mom, Maggie, suffers from dementia. She's ninety-eight years old and, as Kathy said, her sharp mind was her best asset. The grips of that horrible disease have robbed her of that. I know what it feels like to watch a loved one slowly go downhill. I lost my grandma, Elaine Lahren, to dementia two years ago. It's truly the cruelest disease and my heart breaks for anyone who goes through it or has to watch their loved one fight it. Yes, even my archnemesis, Kathy Griffin.

Here's the deal: Life is not about politics. Life is not about who you voted for or what political party you registered with. It's not about any of that crap. Life is about people. Somewhere along the way, we've lost sight of that. We've started looking at everything on the basis of political affiliation and whose "team" we play for. Listen, I am as political as it gets, and Lord knows I will fight for what I believe in, but I do what I do and I fight for what I fight for because I care about people. *All people.* We've gotta get better, as a collective, at separating people from politics. Heading into 2020, it's gonna be hard for all of us, but we have to make an effort. By all means, debate the issues! Don't ever back down from that! Have that fire in your belly but keep the love in your heart. Kathy and I will likely never agree on Trump, the border wall, or anything else. I'm fine with that. I just want her to know I am thinking about her and her mom and praying for them both.

Chapter 8

SET YOUR PRICE TAG.

*Ladies, don't act like victims. Be fighters. You're
not weak. Show 'em you're not to be f'd with. Be
empowered, not whiners.*

Once *The Blaze* lawsuit was settled, I juggled my op-
tions. Was I going to go out on my own? I met with some
investors, but that didn't feel right. Should I go to a network? Fox was talking to me all summer. When they
finally made an offer, it was way too low. I knew my
worth. Still, I hesitated. *I don't have a job now so maybe
I should take it,* I thought. *Even though it's not what I'm
worth, even though I deserve more money, and even
though it's not exactly what I want to do. What if nothing
else comes along*? Many women can relate. They think

if you don't say, "Yes," you're going to insult somebody. If you don't say, "Yes," you're going to seem ungrateful. I had those same emotions, but they didn't last long. When I reflected on the Fox offer, I knew that it didn't feel quite right. I had to say, "No." Most people would think, Well, you don't have a job, so you *should* just take it. Yet, it's just like being single. Should you date the first dude who comes around? No. You shouldn't. The same goes for a job, and I was okay holding out. I'm not a chess piece; I'm a chess player. Let's play.

The truth was that just getting an offer—even one that was too low—from Fox was a big deal. I mean, it's Fox News! Three years earlier, after I left One America and before I took the job at *The Blaze*, I'd had my first viral "Final Thoughts." It was on the Chattanooga terror attack. I called out radical Islam and the media for trying to whitewash terrorists. I also called out Obama for sending our men and women overseas with their hands tied, unable to fight the battle, putting them in danger.

"Bring the fear of God to their desert," I said. As I often do, I said what people were thinking but wouldn't utter out loud for fear of being called an Islamophobe. But I don't care if you call me that, because you know what? You're right! I have a fear of radical Islam. And I'm not afraid to say it. I'm also not afraid to say that there is a problem with Islam. After all, you don't see Jews out there blowing up buildings and making pipe bombs, and you don't see Christians executing people in cages and taking women as sex slaves. You don't see buildings getting shot up because someone drew of a picture of Jesus.

I said all this and more because I wasn't afraid to be honest and direct. Some of the executives at Fox took note and asked to meet with me. I sat across the table from Suzanne Scott, Bill Shine (president of Fox News), and Jay Wallace. Although I was flattered to meet with all those influential people, they didn't make me an offer. I'm not sure I realized it at the time, but I needed to grow. So I went to *The Blaze,* where, despite the chaos, I perfected my craft. I needed that stepping-stone. (Just a side note: we all need those stepping-stones, but so many people think they're going to get to the top by *skipping* stones. You're not. Sorry.) Fast-forward three years after *The Blaze* lawsuit was settled and I was once again entertaining calls from new Fox copresidents Jay and Suzanne, the same executives I had met with earlier. They had seen that the videos I shot in my car with shitty audio were hitting millions. Now they were interested. But their offer was too low.

"This is all we have," they said. But I wasn't going to be lowballed. I knew my worth, and I was bold enough to take a leap of faith. I believed in myself. At the same time, *The Hill* was pursuing me aggressively to do a show out of Los Angeles for much more money. I was excited about it, so we spent almost two months working out the details of the deal. Then, in July, Suzanne asked to meet with me again.

"We know you've got another offer, but we think you'd be great here and we really want you," she said. However, the new offer wasn't much more than the first one. It was about what I had been making at *The Blaze*. I sat up in my chair and looked Suzanne in the eye.

"I'm so grateful that you're offering me what you are. But I've got to be honest with you, Suzanne. I'm a businesswoman, and when your offer is X and the other offer is Y, and they're not even in the same ballpark, I can't do that to myself," I said. "I want to be here, but the difference is too dramatic." She said she understood. We shook hands and I flew back to Dallas later that day after doing a round of shows across Fox and the Fox Business Network.

Guess what? A week later, Fox wanted to have another call. *They're just going to come back with the same lowball offer and try to sweet talk me*, I thought. But when we got on the phone, they said they would match *The Hill*'s offer and meet a list of things I wanted. Now they were in the game. They didn't offer me everything I wanted, but it was enough. They came back to me because I had walked in the room and told another woman who had worked hard and was in a position of power what I was worth. That was a huge moment for me. Power respects power. Women talk about not making as much money as men, but in most cases gender is *not* the issue. It's because we often don't have the balls to go in and demand more money. And no, it's not the "shackles of patriarchy" that inhibits us or our ability to ask for more, it's our lack of confidence. Yeah, most of us have grown up in a "man's world," but it's only a man's world if we are too meek and quiet to rule that world.

Yes, women go through challenges and obstacles in the workplace that men traditionally have not had to, *but,* as a woman, wouldn't you rather push through those challenges and obstacles and come out on the other side like even more of a badass than the men sitting around you? Well, to do that, you're gonna have to stop complaining, stop seeing yourself as a victim, grow some ovaries, and build your confidence. Truth is, if you're a real woman, a man can't give you confidence and he sure as hell can't take it away. Besides, we are in the #MeToo era, so if you're a white, straight, man, it's open season on your ass.

I was thrilled to have two amazing opportunities. But I was also a complete basket case. The *Hill* deal was almost ready to be signed, literally ready for pen to paper, and Fox had come in with another offer. But I wasn't surprised to have two great deals to choose from because I know my worth. I'd said "No" and "No" and "No" and the offers kept coming! Several networks had looked at my Facebook following and saw that it grew from 4.3 million to

almost 4.7 million when I left *The Blaze*. I filmed videos in
my car that were hitting millions—a signal to any network
that this girl doesn't need you, but *you* might need her.

Although I wanted to work for a network because it's
cushy, I realized that I didn't *need* one. I could go out on
my own and be fine. Actually, more than fine. I didn't
"have to do" anything or compromise because I know
my worth. I decided to accept the job at Fox. But first I
wanted to make sure that they knew what they were getting when they hired me. My goal is always to be myself,
honest and straightforward, and some people can't handle
that. For example, Matt and Will were my agents at ICM
when I was at *The Blaze*. All seemed good until one February day when I got a call from Matt.

"ICM told us that we can no longer represent you because the company doesn't feel like you reflect their values," he said.

"What? You guys represent athletes and other personalities who have troubled pasts or scandals but *I'm* too
controversial?" I asked.

"We tried that argument, but they don't want anything
to do with you," Matt said. This was during awards season,
right after the Golden Globes and Meryl Streep's speech,
when I started being vocal about Hollywood. I guess ICM
didn't like that. Lesson learned: know who you are working with and make sure they know who you are. After all,

while I was at *The Blaze*, the *Dallas Morning News* profiled me under the headline "Too Controversial for Fox News." So before I signed anything, I called Suzanne at Fox.

"I'm controversial," I said. "I don't want to come to Fox only to have you tell me what I can and can't say."

"We know you're controversial and we respect that," she said. That was another huge moment, because I didn't just want money in my pocket; I wanted the freedom to be a voice for the voiceless and to be myself, politically incorrect but intellectually honest.

Now, let's be clear: knowing your worth doesn't mean you demand things that you don't deserve or just ask for more and more money. No. It means you work your ass off so you are valuable. When I worked at Express in college, my goal was to be the best salesperson in the whole place. Were my future plans to sell jeans at the mall? Hell no. But as long as I was employed at Express and it was my job, you'd better believe I was going to be the best at it.

There's a quote I've seen: "The way you do one thing is the way you do everything." It's true. The skills you learn in one job—no matter how shitty that job is—and a positive, serious work ethic will carry through to the next one. Look, I didn't go to an Ivy League school, I went to UNLV, which has the highest dropout rate in the country and classes such as Sex, Dance, and Entertainment (which I admit I enrolled in). I see all these kids preparing for college and stressing themselves sick over the accolades on their application and then the school name on their resume. Stop. I can tell you from experience, it's not where you go to school, and it's not the bogus extracurriculars you sign up for to pad your application. It's your work ethic and your ability to talk to people. Heck, I may have learned more about the world selling moderately priced sweaters at Express than I did in four years of journalism school. Why? Two reasons. One, if I'm spending my time doing something, I'm going to do a good job. Two, I hated that job and Lord knows I worked my ass off to make sure I wasn't working retail beyond college. Let circumstances you don't like motivate you to aim (and achieve) better.

I know lots of people who are waiting for a dream job or even just a better job. While they wait, their attitude is "I'm going to be crappy at what I'm doing now to get by, but when I'm finally living my dream, I'll work hard. *That's* when I'll do a good job." In other words, when you become an actress you're going to be great, but in the meantime when you're a server at a restaurant, you're going to be a bitch, not take good care of people, and have an I'm-too-good-for-this air about you. Sorry, that's just not going to cut it. You can't be mediocre at one thing but then expect to shine at what you like to do. That's not how I live my life, because that doesn't pan out in the long run. And it's not what my parents taught me. Was my dad's

dream as a child to grow up and be a building management supervisor for Target Corporation? No. I don't think
so. Was it my mom's dream to be a loan officer at a bank?
Um, probably not. But they are going to be the best at
their jobs they can possibly be. They don't go to work and
think, I've got to get in and get out and just make it until
Friday, a mentality I saw a lot in my hometown.

My parents' goal in life was to raise me in such a way
that I could live out my dreams. They don't get joy out of
their jobs like I do, but they get joy out of watching me do
what I love. Although my parents could probably have
done other things professionally, they've made that huge
sacrifice because they grew up in such a way that it wasn't
about follow your dreams, go smoke weed, be a hippie, be
an artist. They were taught that you need to pay the bills,
you need to take care of your family, and the best product of your life is how you raise your kids. I watched my
parents do what was necessary, not always what was fun.

Even though I love my job, I still do a lot of things that
are necessary but not fun. I do them because I'm setting
myself up for the next thing. For example, sometimes I
do a speech far below my normal fee, and it's on my one
day off. But in those moments the way my parents raised
me kicks in. Yes, it's lower than I normally make, but if
I can speak for half an hour and put that money away for
a rainy day, I'd better do it. Because I know what it's like

to have a rainy day! *The Blaze* lawsuit, coupled with how my parents raised me, taught me that. And when I think about the money, I don't think about a down payment on a house or paying for my wedding. What I really think is that if I can make X amount and use some of that to fly my parents to Los Angeles to come to see and enjoy my life here, I'll do the speech. Or I'll use the money to bring my parents to some of my events.

Last year I brought my dad to an event I did in Milwaukee. Now, Milwaukee in March doesn't sound that great, and it wasn't. It was cold and windy, but for my dad just being able to come with me was such a huge thing that he still talks about it. He appreciates the little things like the meal we ate at the airport restaurant. He was just so happy to go with me. Sometimes, when I'm about to complain about something, I have to take a step back and realize I could be digging a ditch. But instead, I can give a speech for half an hour and make more than my parents make in a week. It's at those times or when I sign someone's MAGA hat or take a picture with them that I think, I am just a girl from South Dakota who worked really, really hard and now I'm here.

I grew up in the middle of the country in a place where it seemed like a lot of people just lived for the weekend. They hated their lives and just muddled through every other day to get to Friday. I've had similar thoughts. I'd think, *I have work today so I can't go out and have fun.* Or when I was obsessive about my eating, I thought, *I can't eat anything bad on Sunday through Thursday. I can only do that on Fridays and Saturdays.* But I think you start living when you realize that you can be happy every single day. Eat cake on Tuesday, have a glass of wine on Wednesday. Who cares? There is no reason not to go out and do at least one thing you want to do every single day. The motto on the whiteboard on my fridge is "Stop acting like you live twice." I think a lot of times we do that. You just go through your day doing things you "have" to do. But if you died tomorrow, would you be happy that was how you spent your last twenty-four hours on this earth? Look, I'm not saying that you're going to Disneyland every day. There are going to be things that you don't want to do, and you're not going to like every part of every day. But you can do something to achieve your goals every day. Have foresight. Look way down the line, not just in front of your face. This will help you achieve those goals, and when you do, you will be able to set that price tag.

I've watched so many of my high school classmates settle for what was easy, not what they truly wanted. Don't do it. There is nothing wrong with staying in your hometown or starting a family, but it's not so much what you do as *why* you do it. Is this the life you wanted or is this the life that was most convenient? Funny thing is, most of these people were far more popular than me in high school. They were the athletes, the dancers, the cool kids who got invited to parties and always had plans on Friday nights. That was enough for them. Not me: Do you want to be the popular girl in high school with all the friends and party invites or do you want to be the twenty-five-year-old making a million dollars a year and continuing to climb? The same girls who made fun of me in high school, and whom my boyfriend cheated on me with, who looked down on me and excluded me, now will approach me at the Rushmore Mall in Rapid City, South Dakota, asking for a photo. Am I better than them? No. Did I give up what I wanted most to be the popular girl in high school? No. Am I happier with the way my life turned out? Hell-to-the-yes.

So are you doing what you want? Or did you settle? If you answered yes, move on. What are you passionate about? Do you light up when you talk about what you're doing? Does it fire you up? Or are you spinning wheels to get a paycheck? Many people have this concept of what they "should" want or aspire to based on other people's desires, what looks good on Instagram, or what society tells them. Now, don't get me wrong, I'm not telling you to "follow your dreams." Someone once told me that's the worst advice you can give a young person and I agree. Why? Because that's the most expensive and naïve thing you can do. Don't follow your dreams. Achieve your goals.

It's because people say "follow your dreams" that you have people waiting tables in LA for twenty years because they're going to be actors "someday." They're following their dreams, but they are not achieving their goals. There's a big difference. Following your dreams means you don't have a plan, don't have a way to sustain yourself, and just fly in the breeze. I'm sorry, but that doesn't pay the bills. We have all these people who are homeless and shoving needles in their arm because they "followed their dreams." Instead achieve your goals, which you do by having a plan, something that's going to get you from point A to point B. You want to be an actress? Great. Set achievable goals and each day do something to work toward achieving them. Get better at them.

Also, know that sometimes your goals are going to cost you. When I graduated from high school, I didn't want to go to a South Dakota school because I knew that my opportunities for the future would be limited. Instead I chose a university that was more expensive, *but* I knew what I was getting into. My parents are not rich, so, although they helped me out, I largely paid my college tuition through student loans. I also worked hard at a part-time job from sophomore through senior year to get residency to make my tuition cheaper. My point is that you need to have foresight. I don't think about what's right in front of me. It would have been easier to go to a state school, pay almost nothing, get a degree, and *then* figure out where I wanted to go. But I knew that would stunt me and that going to UNLV would place more opportunities at my fingertips and set me up for a job when I graduated that would help me pay back those loans.

You can do anything you want in life and make any choice you want to make, but you have to be able to accept the consequences. People go to expensive schools that they can't afford and then complain about not being able to pay off the debt. But you can't act like you didn't get yourself into that situation. It's like going to a Mercedes dealership when you have a Prius budget and saying you want a Mercedes, but you don't know how the hell you're going to pay for it. I'm not saying you can't go to those schools, but you'd better have a way, a plan, for how you're going to pay for it. And if you're not prepared, then go to a community college or go to a vocational school or get a job that you think is going to best set you up to achieve your goals five to ten years from now. Don't let your life situation and your financial situation limit you. Don't go for the option that's cheapest for now or to the best party school. If you know that your track isn't to go to college and be a biologist and you'd rather do hair, go to cosmetology school. You don't need to go to a four-year school so that you can say you went to a four-year school. Don't do things based on the perception of others. Do it based on your plan, your long-term goals, and what you think you can feasibly achieve. Then push yourself to get it. I always knew in the back of my mind that I'd have to pay off those student loans—loans that I *just* paid off last week!—and I didn't complain to anyone because I got myself into that situation. I got me there. I chose it. No one sprung it on me at the last minute. And a side note to all those college students who bitch and moan about student loans. You insist higher education should be free? Then I'd better not see your ass headed to Cancun for spring break with a five-dollar Starbucks drink, hundred-dollar Lululemon leggings, and some Apple AirPods in your ears!

You need to think about what you want and then set those goals. I have gone through waves of that in my life where I have taken a step back and thought, *What do I truly want? I'm doing everything and I'm chugging along, but what is my end goal?* You have to do this even when you're in a great place. For example, I got to Fox News, which was a huge accomplishment. I launched Fox Nation, another huge one. But where do I want to be a year from now? Two years from now? I don't want to be in the same place or have the same goals. You have to keep moving the goalposts or otherwise you stay comfortable. To me, the definition of failure is not losing your job, going broke or bankrupt, or getting divorced. It's sitting here in a year and being in the same position that I am in right now. Failure is staying in the same spot because it's comfortable and safe to spin your wheels and simply go through the motions.

Knowing your price tag doesn't just apply to business or job negotiations. This applies to your personal life just as much as your professional life. Most of my friends are thirty-three to thirty-five years old. One of them just went through the process of having her eggs frozen because she's been so focused on her career, she's concerned that she's not going to find someone. At almost thirty-six, this is a reality for her. But here's the thing. This friend of mine has this very extensive checklist (that most women have) and any guy she'll date has to check every box: have a good job, wear a suit to work, make a certain amount of money, have gone to a certain school, dress a certain way, be tall, etc. Well, she was recently dating someone who fit everything on her list. It all seemed perfect. That was, until she got an email from a girl on Facebook who said, "Your boyfriend has been reaching out to a lot of people on Tinder, including myself, saying he wants to meet up." Unfortunately, this wasn't the only girl she heard from, and when she confronted her boyfriend, he didn't even deny it. The lowest blow of all was that he said he wasn't attracted to her anymore. A total cop-out.

My friend was devastated. She called me in tears. "At

my age, I'm not going to find anyone and get married and have a family," she said, with her voice cracking. "And if I do meet a guy, I'm going to have to have kids the next day because I'm getting older." The fact that this girl who has a terrific job, comes from a great family, and is an amazing person can be reduced to rubble based on some asshole is astounding to me. I don't blow smoke up my friends' asses, though, so I was straight with her. I told her that I *did* think she was going to find someone, but that her mile-long checklist was not only unreasonable but eliminated most of the world's potential suitors. I'm not saying lower your standards and don't worry about knowing what you want in life, but part of setting your price tag is setting yourself up for success.

I understand what it's like to have a type. I'm someone who used to only date six-foot-tall Navy SEALs with six-pack abs or country music stars. But your type doesn't matter. You need to go with the person who lights you up every day, the person who knows your worth. Who cares what he wears? You can buy him a suit! If he is a police officer and loves his job or owns a supersuccessful plumbing company and he treats you right and lights you up, you can take him shopping! Don't limit yourself. Set your price tag, but don't automatically discount other people if they don't fit your checklist. Give people a chance. Get out of your comfort zone. Of course, yes, have standards and expectations, but don't be afraid to color outside the lines sometimes. The other night I was at a girls' dinner with some friends. One of the girls was sharing her hilarious hookup stories but simultaneously complaining about being thirty-one years old, single, and childless. I couldn't help but ask if she tends to sleep with guys on the first date. Unsurprisingly, she said yes, that was her norm. Often women do this for the feeling of affection, intimacy, and attention—but not this girl. She insisted she simply likes sex and doesn't feel like she should have to pick one or the other. In fact, she was upset women are often made to feel dirty for that desire while men celebrate it. I get it, but here's what I told her. Yes, it may suck women have to take it slower for men to value us. It may not seem fair. Life isn't fair. You might want to eat cupcakes all day and be skinny and fit but guess what? That's not gonna happen either! Life is often about delayed gratification. You might want it, whatever *it* is, but do you really want to give up a better thing for what you want in the moment?

Whether we like it or not, our value is constantly assessed by others. The trick is to set your price tag and teach people how to treat you. Are you putting yourself on the clearance rack by being lazy? Well, don't be surprised when you're treated like a blue light special.

Chapter 9

YOU *ARE* ENOUGH.

You will be too much for some people.
Those aren't your people.

Although I'm blessed to have two great parents who are incredibly strong and stable, every family goes through stuff and mine was no exception. When I was around ten years old, we went over to my grandparents' house for dinner. When we walked into the living room, there was my mom's dad, Grandpa Dietrich, sitting on the couch in his underwear. No shirt. No shoes. Just underwear. *What is Grandpa doing?* I wondered. Then out of nowhere, he started to tell stories from his childhood and growing up during the Great Depression. He was slurring his words. My parents were not drinkers, their friends were not drinkers, and neither were my other family members, so I'd never seen anyone in that state before. In that moment, I realized that my grandpa was an alcoholic. Up until then, I thought my family was perfect. My parents never fought and had been married for twenty years, and the three of us were as tight-knit as you could be. My grandparents were married for more than fifty years and no one in my extended family, with the exception of my mom's sister, was divorced. Plus, my four cousins and I were really close.

After that day, my grandpa's drinking just got worse and my parents didn't shield me from it. (They always treated me like an adult and were very open with me, which I think is one reason I've always been able to manage things in my life.)

I learned my grandpa had severe depression and would try to numb the pain by drinking. There were many nights when he would get so drunk that my grandma couldn't take it a second longer. She would come to our house to spend the night, something that became a normal part of my life. At one point, she rented her own little place in town. She's one of the strongest people I know, but eventually she went back to him.

My grandpa and dad were the best of friends, so many nights my grandpa would call our house drunk and ask my dad to get him some whiskey.

"I can't do that," my dad would say.

"Then I'll get it myself," my grandpa would respond. Not wanting him to drive drunk, my dad would then have to drive the half hour to my grandparents' house and spend the night talking to my grandpa. One time my grandpa threatened to kill himself. Worried that he'd do something reckless, my family members called the sheriff.

I didn't have close friends growing up, but I never told the few that I *did* have or anyone else that my grandpa was an alcoholic. I was very embarrassed. Right before my middle school graduation, my grandma was staying with us on an almost nightly basis.

"If Grandma is going to come to my graduation, she can't talk about Grandpa's drinking," I told my parents. I worried that people outside our family would find out.

After that, my grandpa went to rehab for three months and was completely sober for six years, until my sophomore year of college. He also found God. It was such a turning point for him and our family. In the end, even his faith wouldn't prevent tragedy, but knowing he is in heaven is a comfort for my family.

Despite his drinking, I always looked up to my grandpa because he was one of the hardest-working people I knew. He and my grandma got married when they were just sixteen years old and had their first child, my uncle, the same year. They lived in a trailer on a ranch where my grandpa worked incredibly hard. With just an eighth-grade education, he built a multimillion-dollar ranch from nothing. My grandma, who didn't graduate from high school, helped him and together were two of the hardest-working and most resilient people I knew. It was a very tough time and there was an incredible amount of pressure to make it.

Although my grandpa was very successful, he always strived to be better. I think it's because he grew up during the Depression and with a father who was an abusive alcoholic. From the time he was a young child, his father would tell him that he wasn't good enough. He wasn't tough enough or smart enough. His dad didn't shower him with compliments. My grandpa was brilliant, had a great family, and built an incredibly successful business from the ground up, but it was never enough, and his depression kicked in especially hard when he felt inadequate.

My grandpa was also a fun-loving prankster. He and I were especially close because we shared a love of politics. It was something we bonded over. Grandpa had Fox News on the television 24/7 with the volume up so loud that my grandma was constantly yelling, "Turn that down!" *She* didn't like it, but I loved it. I remember being at their house and watching *Hannity & Colmes*. My grandpa also loved Glenn Beck. (Funny how things come full circle!)

In fact, he used to call my house to make sure my parents were recording Glenn Beck for me.

When I was a freshman in college and heard there was going to be a Glenn Beck Tea Party rally in Rapid City, South Dakota, I volunteered to work it so I could get tickets for my grandpa and me. My job was to bring people up to Glenn to take pictures.

"Make sure you tell him that I'm his biggest fan," my grandpa said. And I did. That was a special moment for us, especially because one year to the day of that rally, my grandpa committed suicide. (This is why getting the job at *The Blaze* five years later was so significant. It was a connection with my grandpa, who would have been so disappointed to learn who Glenn Beck *really* was.)

In October of my sophomore year of college, I was in my apartment at UNLV when my phone rang. It was my mom.

"Grandpa shot himself," she said. *What?* I was stunned. I knew he struggled with depression, but I had no idea that he had started drinking again. My parents and grandmother knew and tried to stop him.

"Don't worry. In three more days, it'll be okay," he told them. Then, "In two more days, it'll be okay." My family thought he just needed to get through this depression, but he was counting down until he was going to kill himself. Just three days from when he started to drink again, he shot himself in my grandparents' bedroom. Apparently he stopped taking his antidepressants because he hated how tired they made him feel. Unfortunately, his depression got bad again, which is what made him fall off the wagon. He loved life, but he loved being a success more, and he thought his return to drinking would disappoint and burden our family. This was too much for him to handle.

I flew back to Rapid City the next day for the funeral, which was on Halloween. That was a tough time for my whole family—especially for my dad. They all knew that my grandpa had started drinking again, but not how bad it was. Every day my dad would call my grandma.

"How is he doing?" he'd ask.

"He's drinking, but he's fine," she'd say. But he wasn't fine. And honestly, my dad is convinced to this day that if my grandma had told him how bad it really was, he could have gone down there and saved him. I'm not sure if that's true, but I know that my dad lives with that every single day. Some part of him will always hold it against my grandma. It's not obvious when we're together, but he doesn't like going to her house for family events and I don't think he will ever forgive her for that and for being so callous after his death.

When my grandpa shot himself, my grandma was in town having lunch with my mom and aunt. She came home to him dead on their bedroom floor. But she just cleaned up the blood and slept in there that night. What the hell? All of us were shocked. It was mystifying. Grandma didn't even seem to be mourning. She almost seemed relieved. They had a horrible relationship and shouldn't have been together. My grandma did everything, but my grandpa was very hard on her. He would tell her that she wasn't good enough, not a good enough cook, not a good enough cleaner.

I didn't understand it at the time, but now I know that when someone is attacking you, it's because of their *own* insecurity. My grandpa didn't feel that *he* was good enough, so what did he do? He projected it on my grandma. I don't blame her for feeling a sense of relief when he passed away. It might not sound good, but sometimes the truth doesn't sound good or even make you feel good—it just is.

On the way back from the funeral, my cousins were talking about not telling people that Grandpa committed suicide. Most of them were ashamed. At first I was a little embarrassed, too. Suicide was not discussed publicly the way it is today and most people don't lose a grandparent that way. It's not always easy to talk about, but I decided to be open. Keeping it to myself wouldn't help anybody; talking about it just might. I dedicated my "Final Thoughts" to telling the story both at my first show on

One America and again on my show at *The Blaze*. Even the best families go through stuff. We should be able to have a conversation about it.

MY GRANDPA COMMITTED suicide because he never felt good enough. This resonates with me in every area of my life because I have his type A personality. That's why I work so hard to stay grounded and count my blessings: I know how quickly it can consume you. My grandpa was never famous, but he felt like he needed to accumulate all this money or else he would not be good enough. His motivation wasn't greed; it was a need for validation. Sometimes I think that if I'm not doing X, Y, and Z then I'm not good enough. I've heard it from former bosses. I've heard it from the left. And I've heard it from the right. I've heard it from total strangers (lots of them) on social media. I've been told I'm not smart enough, I'm not pretty enough, and I'm not conservative enough. I'm not educated enough or polished enough. I've been told, "You went to a shitty school, so why are you an expert on this?" You name it, someone has told me that I'm not enough of it. That's why having confidence in yourself is so important. I saw that my grandpa didn't have that. He was brilliant and built something from nothing. He worked from the ground up and was incredibly success-ful but it didn't matter. It was never enough. He was on a never-ending search to fill that hole and he ended his life empty because of it.

However, people who want to change you are usually people who are trying to avoid fixing themselves.

Because of my grandpa's depression and suicide, I now mentor several girls whom I call my "number ones." There are three in particular. I talk to them daily on Instagram, and they know they can DM me day or night. They've been my biggest fans for the longest time and will drive hours to come to my events. One is Sydney, a twenty-two-year-old who struggled with depression and drug addiction. Then a friend told her about my "Final Thoughts."

"They made me realize that I had to stop acting like a victim and take ownership of my life and the choices I was making," Sydney said. She worked hard to turn her life around and now she is completely clean and sober. Always interested in politics, she used some of the stuff I said on "Final Thoughts" to debate with her friends, and this helped her find a purpose. Today she writes political blogs, some of which I retweet. Her friend Cathy is also one of my "number ones." She is currently struggling with depression and reaches out to me to share her difficult but honest thoughts. She recently came out as a conservative and found that a lot of her friends turned on her.

The third girl, Ellie, was a high schooler who reached out when her school's administration came down on her for posting conservative videos. They tried to make her take them down, but she refused. I reposted some of them, and she got an amazing response. Weeks later, her boyfriend told me that she had just admitted herself to the hospital for bipolar depression and suicidal thoughts. I tried to help her through it by telling her about my grandpa and said I know what it feels like. I told her not to be ashamed or embarrassed. In the end, she pushed through it and ended up going to military school and then getting into a good university to study politics.

It's so important to me to mentor these girls because I realize the impact that I can have, and it's one I take very, very seriously. I don't care about recognition from conservative websites or bloggers or the media. I care about recognition from girls like these because I wouldn't be here without them. They message me when they are having tough times, and I try to help get them through with a text or inspirational quote and help them find their purpose. And honestly, they help me and inspire me more than I help them. On my darkest, most stressful days, when someone is going after me on Twitter or I'm frustrated at work, they remind me why I do what I do. Being there for them also helps me deal with the loss of my grandpa and reminds me that we all have something in common.

SOMETIMES THE WAY you grow up makes you used to bad things. Something that ought to be a deal breaker seems normal to you.

At the time of my grandfather's death, I was dating my first boyfriend, Brian. We'd been together for four years at this point, and I wasn't happy. Watching how my grandmother reacted made me think; it clicked for me: I couldn't be with Brian anymore. I didn't want to have a relationship like my grandparents' and yet I was headed in that direction. I could see that pattern.

Brian and I dated for six years starting in my sophomore year of high school. Brian was a cocky, entitled star baseball player—or at least that was the front he put up. As a baseball player who can throw the ball 90-plus mph, he was a big fish in the small pond of Rapid City. After all, we only had two main high schools, and the whole town was just 70,000 people. But I knew Brian, and I mean really *knew* him. Behind his star athlete persona, he was incredibly insecure. His parents loved him, but they seemed to love him even more when he did well in baseball. It was obvious, but he would never admit it or how much this hurt him. That is why he became attached-at-the-hip close with my dad, who tried to mentor him on how to be a good man. My dad couldn't care less if Brian did well in baseball or even played baseball. My whole family saw and cared about the person he was regardless of sports. That's why I never broke up with him, even when he was mean and condescending, constantly telling me that I was nothing and dragging me down. He would belittle me and my dreams.

He also cheated on me so many times—three times in high school alone—he put me and my confidence through the wringer.

As confident as I was academically and professionally, my personal confidence came much later.

I would make excuses for him, telling myself, *That wasn't the real Brian who did that to you, that was the fake Brian putting on a show.* I also kept getting back together with him because he was my first boyfriend and best friend and, good or bad, he had shaped a lot of my life. I knew when I was sixteen years old that this relationship was not going to work out, but I held on to it and held on to it. I should never have stuck around as long as I did, but I loved him unconditionally. (When I say I am loyal to a fault, this is the perfect example.)

I also wasn't strong enough to walk away. And Brian preyed on that. In fact, toward the end of our relationship

Brian knew I was on the way out the door; he could feel it. So what did he do? He would call me and insinuate he may hurt himself. He knew this would have a dramatic impact on me because of my grandpa. He used it to control me. He still cheated on me numerous times, which was not only painful but embarrassing, because everyone at school knew before I did. The mean girls thought it was funny to say things about it to me.

If we find someone who tells us what we want to hear, we fall in love with that feeling, not always with that person. And we do whatever is needed to hold on to it. That was me. Sometimes it doesn't matter if the person is condescending and horrible 90 percent of the time. We hold onto that somewhat decent 10 percent. I admit, I held on to that 10 percent for way too long. Now it's such a disappointment for me to look back on that experience, because I can't believe I let someone have such a hold over me.

WHEN WE GRADUATED from high school, we both went to UNLV for college. Brian got a baseball scholarship and I was going to study journalism. The first week I felt totally alone, and Brian was nowhere to be found. He was too busy with his new baseball friends, while I didn't know anyone. Getting to play Division 1 baseball is a huge accomplishment—especially when you come from a small town—so he was super cocky about being on the team, and he was treating me like crap.

"I am king shit around here," he told me. "I'll stay with you because I feel sorry for you, but just know I'll probably cheat on you," he said. That was his way of dumping me while still holding on in case he needed me. I had to untangle myself from him and the only way to do that was to leave UNLV. If I didn't make a big move and stop the pattern, it would never end. (Yes, we got back together, *but* when you're with someone for years and you practically grow up with them, it takes a few good-byes before the final one.) I called my mom.

"If I stay here, I'm going to fall back into this relationship because it's comfortable," I said.

So, just five days after my parents had moved me into my dorm, my mother flew to Vegas to help me move out. I went back to South Dakota and enrolled in a local engineering school for the first semester of my freshman year and lived at home for a few months before heading back to UNLV for the spring semester.

I thought people would view it as me running back home, but it wasn't. I had been with Brian for two and a half years. By leaving I was saying, "I can't do this anymore. This cycle has to end, and the only way is if

I leave." Well, guess what? As soon I left, Brian would call me bawling about how he couldn't get through school without me.

"I need you," he'd cry into the phone. Even his parents got involved.

"Tomi, can you please go back to Vegas because Brian can't do this without you?" they said. What did I do? I spent my own money to fly to Vegas and stay in a hotel room so that I could visit him four times during that first semester. We got back together. Little did I know, he was cheating on me that whole time and not only that, but bragging about it in the locker room. One of his baseball teammates later told me Brian would boast about how many times he'd cheated on me and how pathetic I was for continuing to come and see him in Vegas.

AT THAT POINT, it was like an appendage, like a tumor. I knew he was so bad for me, but the pain of removing the tumor was scary. It seemed worse than the pain of being *in* the relationship. On top of that, I loved him. Since then, I've learned that true maturity is being able to love somebody even though they may not love you back. But I wasn't there yet.

I decided to go back to UNLV for spring semester.

"I feel really bad about everything that I did. Can we go find our classes together before the semester starts?" he asked.

"Okay." After walking around campus, we drove to get groceries. We were in Brian's car when the girl he cheated with called. His phone was connected to Bluetooth, so the whole conversation was on speaker. And it gets better: the girl told him that she thought she was pregnant, and he was arguing with her and telling her she needed to get an abortion. *Where am I?* I thought. When they hung up, Brian broke down crying because he was so worried about her having the baby.

"Baseball will be over for me, and my parents will be so disappointed," he cried. "Can you call my dad and tell him?" Yes. The truth is stranger than fiction. And guess what? I did it. I called his dad!

"Brian is terrified to tell you this, but he thinks he got a girl pregnant and he doesn't know what to do," I told him.

"I need to talk to him," his dad said. So, I sat there as they talked on the phone about another girl being pregnant. *This is the worst*, I thought. But *again* I stepped in to take care of him. It turns out that the girl was lying about the whole thing.

You would think I would have ended it there, but no, we continued to date for three and a half more years. By the time we were sophomores, Brian had so many injuries that he could no longer play baseball. He went to college thinking that he was going to get drafted, so this was devastating to him and that's when his emotional attacks on me got worse. Funny, because when he was on top of the world, he treated me like shit, and then when things started to unravel he *still* treated me like shit. It just goes to show that a crappy person is a crappy person and people are either going to treat you well or they're not. Their behavior is not always dependent on the situation.

Without baseball and his teammates, Brian lost his identity and became clingy and possessive. He wanted to hang out all the time, but I was going to school full-time and working a retail job at Express. By the end of the day, I was tired and didn't want to be around anyone. Still, he'd pressure me to come over. It was a control thing for him, something I didn't realize at the time. When I did hang out with him, I would literally count the minutes until I could leave. And the thought of Brian physically touching me repulsed me. I just wanted out. This was no way to live, yet I felt like I couldn't get out of this relationship. Anytime I tried to break up with Brian, he'd go into a dark and depressed state, something he knew would work to keep me because it was just a year after my grandpa ended his own life. This brought me back to that awful time. People find your triggers and exploit you, and that's what Brian did. He was trying to use the biggest tragedy in my life to manipulate me. I don't even know if he realized how hard it was on me. I loved the guy. I truly did. Part of me will always love him. It wasn't easy to walk away. It was one of the hardest things I have ever done.

I know a lot of people are in the position I was in and it's not easy. Although I knew that I didn't want to be with Brian, I also knew that he was going to act irrationally if I broke up with him. I stayed with him longer and longer because I didn't want to have to deal with his reaction. I had seen his anger issues earlier in our relationship. For example, freshman and sophomore year, if his coach didn't put him in to play during a baseball game, he'd be so mad that he'd take it out on me afterward. He'd call me every name in the book. He'd slam doors and punch holes in walls.

Finally, in March of my junior year, I couldn't take it anymore. After two years of trying to get out of that relationship, I broke up with Brian for good. Of course, he didn't make it easy. He would text me so many times in a row that my phone would physically shut down. He lived across from me in the same apartment complex, so he would stand at the window and wait for my car to pull in. Then he'd send me nasty texts. He even insinuated he might do something to my car or slash my tires. He followed me to the gym, trying to convince me to change my mind. It was bad. Once he was done playing baseball, he didn't have an identity anymore and he took all that out on me. He tried to control me and for a long time it worked. But once I broke up with him, he lost control and he went apeshit. After I broke up with him, I never thought he was going to physically hurt me, but I knew he wouldn't leave me alone. I threatened to get a restraining order, something I really didn't want to do. I didn't want to ruin his life. I just wanted him to get the hell out of mine. I took matters into my own hands. When school was out, I decided to go home that summer before my senior year.

Looking back, I realize that Brian was insecure about his intelligence. His parents put so much weight into him being a baseball player and didn't give him the confidence that he could do anything else. He was lost and insecure. He had to put me down to build himself him up. He cheated on me because he was insecure and needed validation.

Brian was my best friend, and I won't take that away from him. I owe a lot of the fact that I never partied or drank in high school to Brian, because we did everything together. But his verbal abuse affected my confidence. It got into my head. Because Brian couldn't control his injuries or baseball, he tried to control me and projected his insecurities on me. And it worked. I didn't realize it until I was out of the relationship, which is something that happens to a lot of women—even strong, successful women.

People are always surprised when I tell them about Brian and the way that I allowed him to treat me. They think it wouldn't happen to me because I'm so confident in myself, but you aren't always confident in all areas of your life. Today I would never put up with that, but it took a lot of reflection to figure it out. I always thought, *No one is going to make me do this or that*, so I didn't *think* he had control over me, but looking back I realize he had an immense amount. Sometimes it's just not as blatant and obvious, especially when you are young or you think you love someone.

HERE'S ANOTHER ISSUE involving someone else telling you you're not enough: you can take it to heart long after they're gone. You hear their voice in your head. Brian used to tease me and call me names like "tubble-ump-kin" and question what I was eating. Although I wasn't overweight at all, he got so deep into my head that I always thought I was. It bothered me, so when I finally broke up with him my confidence was at an all-time low. *I am going to get really skinny,* I thought. Now *I* was in control, but I took it overboard. That's when I started running. At first it was a very positive and healthy thing for me, but I became obsessive about it. I also became obsessive about food. I would calculate what I ate down to the last ingredient and had a very calorie-restrictive diet. Although I was eating healthy, I was not eating enough, and I was running seven miles a day. By the summer after my junior year, I was under 100 pounds. At five feet four, that's way too skinny, something I couldn't see. On my twenty-first birthday, my grandma said, "Tomi, you look like you're in one of those world hunger commercials." I was so mad and devastated. Other people said things to me, too, but I just got defensive. I couldn't see the problem.

Yes, it can be helpful to know what you're eating, and it's important to choose healthy foods, but I got crazy about it. I was at the point where I'd eat almost nothing all day and then gorge myself at the end of the night. I was often lightheaded and dizzy. I also stopped going out with friends, because I was afraid that if there was something like pizza in front of me, I'd eat it. And if I did succumb to foods that weren't on my rigid plan, I'd beat myself up and feel like a failure.

I was super skinny all through senior year, but my confidence slowly began to come back when I started hosting a show called *The Scramble* for UNLV TV in the second semester of my senior year. Then I started working in San Diego, where I began making friends and going out more, something I couldn't do *and* live in my restrictive world. Eventually I realized that I had to live my life and that sometimes you have to break your routine. Slowly

I gained the weight back and stopped obsessing. I still don't like to miss days of running, but I eat what I damn please. It's mostly healthy, but if I eat something that's not, I don't beat myself up over it. When I started to get more personal strength and let go of the mind block that ruled my life, I got over it. Finally I stopped hearing Brian say I wasn't good enough and instead heard myself say that I was.

Although it wasn't as bad or traumatic as my relationship with Brian, the boyfriend I had after college also made me feel less-than. I met him when I moved to San Diego for One America. He was a Navy SEAL named Jason. He was with me when my career was taking off. Even though I was always proud and excited about *his* accomplishments, he made me feel like mine were no big deal. No matter what I did, I could not impress him. Anytime something really exciting happened in my life, he made me feel insecure about it. For example, when I found out that I was in a Jay-Z song, I called him.

"Oh my God. I'm in a Jay-Z song!" I told him excitedly. "I just sent it to you. Listen to it!"

"Oh. Cool," he said halfheartedly. "I'm going out with my friends now. I'll listen later." Of course, he never listened. He had the same lackluster reaction when I said I was going to a Dallas Cowboys dinner with Tony Romo, and when I came home elated about my first paid speech.

I wanted to share these things with him, but he acted like he didn't care. It was so deflating. I felt like he wasn't proud of me and this left me feeling very insecure.

Instead of getting excited and feeling proud about accomplishments that were important to *me*, he focused on all the things I wasn't. I wasn't outdoorsy, I didn't want to go camping, I couldn't be at one event of his because I was working. I could not figure out why I wasn't good enough. And then he dumped me. Twice! On the phone! You can imagine how *that* made me feel.

I knew for a long time Jason and I weren't right for each other, but I always defended his character by saying he never cheated on or betrayed me. Plot twist! At a friend's wedding in San Diego just months ago, I was told by mutual friends that Jason did, in fact, cheat on me. It gets worse. Not only did he cheat on me, the girl he cheated with revealed to *my* friend she knew about me the whole time. In fact, she would drive him to the airport to come see me in Dallas. Yeah, finding that out after over two years of telling people he never cheated makes me feel like a jackass. Now I see that he was incredibly insecure, but when you're *in* it, you think that the problem is all you.

I HAVEN'T SHARED these very personal and painful stories with a lot of people, but I'm sharing them now to make a point: You may have been in a bad situation or had someone do destructive things to you, but nothing is black-and-white. There are bright points and dark points to everything, and you can learn from any situation. Even awful ones. Not just bad boyfriends. I still think of my time at *The Blaze* as an incredible opportunity and one I learned a lot from. At my one-year anniversary at Fox, I thought about how I got there and realized that *The Blaze* provided the stepping-stone that I needed. It wasn't easy, but it was necessary. The same goes not only for everyone who has fired me and put me through a lawsuit, but those who have dumped me like Jason or cheated on me like Brian. Although these experiences were difficult and painful, they were so formative that I wouldn't take back any of them. I learned so much. The most powerful lesson is to reflect on everything and to find out why something is bothering you, why it's a trigger. For example, there are still times when I have dreams about Brian and I know it has nothing to do with him. It's my inner insecurity that's still there. When conservatives say on Twitter that I'm not smart enough and that I'm where I am because I'm pretty, I ask myself, why is that a trigger for me? Because Brian would tell me that I was not good enough.

I'm grateful for every single one of those things, because that's why I am where I am today. If I hadn't been through those things and learned to fight for what I wanted, I might have become a woman who still allows people to tell her how to talk, act, think, dress, and live. I've been there and learned from that behavior and I won't tolerate it anymore. I know the red flags and I avoid going down rabbit holes. If I hadn't been through those things and learned to fight for what I wanted, I might have been one of many conservatives who, when they're told, "We don't want you to do this" or "You're too controversial," fold to the pressure. But now I know this is who I am and this is what I want. I don't regret anything I've done because every misstep I've made and person I trusted (wrongly) have led me to where I am and all the good things that I have in my life now.

Sometimes you don't realize that you have toxic people in your life because you think you can change them. You can't. I have a friend whose cheating boyfriend is in therapy to try to change his ways. You may be the inspiration for him to go to therapy, but you don't have to stay with him. I've also learned that you cannot control other people; all you can do is control your reaction and know when to get out. I used to think that if I was watching Brian all the time and looking at his phone, somehow I could prevent him from cheating on me. But you're not going to keep a liar from lying, you're not going to keep a crook from being a crook, and you're not going to keep a cheater from cheating. Brian is the perfect example. We spoke a few months ago for the first time in four years. I have the same number I had in high school, so he texted me.

"Sorry if you've been trying to reach out to me. I discovered that my wife blocked your number in my phone." Um, no. Still, I wished him well and we spoke on the phone to catch up on each other's lives. I have nothing against him now and only wish him the best.

"I brag about you to people all the time and tell them that I dated you," he said. "Isn't it funny I used to say you were going to be nothing? And now look where you are." Funny how things work out, isn't it? Then he told me that he googled my net worth, too. "I should have held on because you could have been my sugar mama," he said. *You piece of shit. Now you're impressed?*

The next day, Brian texted me again and it didn't take long to realize he hadn't changed a bit. *What if I didn't have the courage to walk away from him?* I thought. *I'd be that girl.* At first I wasn't good enough and I needed his praise and now I just feel sorry for him. He's always on the lookout for bigger and better things. It made me thankful that God showed me the way out of that relationship years ago. Yes, he jolted me out of it, but sometimes it has to get *that* bad because if it doesn't, you're not going to leave. If it doesn't, you're not going to change. He is someone else's concern now, and I wish them the best of luck.

One thing I realized is that you shouldn't wait to be

proud of yourself only after you succeed. Be proud of who you are, and it will *help you succeed.* The bottom line is this: Don't listen when someone tells you that you're not enough. Don't ever let that seep into your brain. Don't let anyone ever tell you that you're not smart enough, pretty enough, fun enough, or whatever enough. Don't let them tell you that you are where you are because of your looks or connections or that you didn't go to a good enough school. Don't ever let anyone reduce you, because when you do, you give them power. And the truth is this: the reason they're saying you're not enough is that you're *too* enough and it scares them. That's *their* problem, not yours!

Chapter 10

TRUST GOD'S PLAN.

Proud of where I come from.
Blessed to be where I am.

My faith was tested when I was going through *The Blaze* lawsuit. I had moved to Dallas specifically for that job, so I had no family around and few friends. My *Blaze* coworkers I'd gotten friendly with couldn't talk to me because of their nondisclosure agreements. To say it was a very lonely time is an understatement. What didn't help were the comments I got from strangers. One time my boyfriend came to visit from San Diego and we were sitting outside of Yogurtland in Irving, Texas. A shitty car passed by and the driver screamed out the window.

"Hey, Tomi! How does it feel not to have a fucking job?" he said. And he wasn't the only one. When I'd tweet about politics, like the firing of FBI director James Comey or Syria, people would comment, "Are you living in your parents' basement?" or "Hey girl with no job!" Now, I don't care how confident you are: things like that can make you feel like a total loser. There were times I'd be crying on the phone to my mom, saying, "Why is this happening? Why am I being put through this hell? I've never done anything to any of these people." I was at the highest point of my career doing my show every day, Fox once a week, and getting interviewed by media outlets like the *New York Times, GQ, Elle,* and *Nightline.* The president of the United States had called *me* to thank me for my videos. But *The Blaze* was forcing me to be silent and wouldn't let me out of their grasp. I didn't want revenge. I didn't want to hurt anybody. I didn't want to ruin Glenn Beck.

"Why isn't this ending the way it's supposed to? Why are they doing this?" I asked my mom.

"Stop questioning your journey," she said. And she was right. Every single step of my life so far, God has led me where I needed to go. I had to remind myself that God prepared me for the lawsuit and that I could handle it. He was telling me that someone needed to be strong enough to call this person out and say, "The emperor has no clothes." God does not put you through stuff you can't handle. It's a test of your true grit.

I'm a proud Christian and child of God, but I'm not church-every-Sunday religious. Growing up, my dad taught me to pray, something he does on his way to work every day, and I always had a relationship with God. But I didn't feel bad about things like swearing, listening to rap music, or being politically pro-choice—because of my religion. That's all bogus. I think God wants me to be a good person, to do the right thing, to be kind to people, and to live a life of Christ. To me, religion isn't about not eating this, not doing that, or even going to church all the time. I think *man* made rituals, not God. I don't believe in the arbitrary rulebook set up by the religious hierarchy. That's not God; that's man pretending to be God. If that offends you, get used to it. That's life. Not every Christian looks at life the same way. I won't apologize for my faith and you shouldn't, either.

During difficult times in my life that I would stress and lose sleep over, my parents always said, "Pray about it, and God will take care of you." They taught me to do the best that *I* can, to work hard and then ask God to take care of the rest. And he always has. I believe the minute you think you can handle everything yourself, that's when you fall. But if you let go, God will lead the way. When my dad quit his job, he didn't know what he was going to do—especially after working for one company for twenty-six years. That's all he knew. He didn't have a college diploma, a trust fund, or a rich uncle to fall back on. But he did everything he possibly could, and then he let God take over, and he found the Target Corporation. Sometimes you have to be patient, because life is about *his* timing, not yours. Of course, that's not always easy, especially for someone as impatient as I am. But you have to trust that he always knows the right thing and will prepare you for what's coming next.

Whenever I have feelings of worry, anxiety, and insecurity, I remember something my dad says all the time: the moment you start to overanalyze stuff, that's an insult to God, because you're telling him that *he* can't handle your life.

I'm not saying you should sit back and be lazy and expect good things to happen for you. But when you have done everything you can, give it to God. My true confidence comes from knowing there's something bigger than me that's watching over me. If you don't have a sense of God, then the weight of the world is on *your* shoulders. So, don't doubt him. Many people think prayer, faith, and worship are about asking for things in tough times. That shouldn't be the only time you look to God. Instead, thank him when things go right, and you're in a good place. Appreciate and enjoy that time. Don't take it for granted. I did that with *The Blaze*. When I was there, I focused on how much I hated it and how badly they treated us, but now I look back and realize what a great opportunity it was in my life. I had my daily show on which I had the freedom to say whatever I wanted—which I don't even have now—but I didn't fully appreciate it. Looking back, I took that time for granted.

You should also thank God when you think things are going wrong but they're actually going right. I know that because I've been there. I can't think of one devastation in my life or one letdown that hasn't turned out to be a blessing or, at the very least, a teaching moment for me. I've been fired, dumped, and cheated on and I'm grateful even for the messy parts.

Know that God will take you where you *need* to go, even if it's not where you *want* to go. We all have that defining moment, that transition time between jobs, relationships, or any other aspect of life where you don't know what's next but have to move forward. That's when you need to remind yourself of God's plan. The next three months are probably going to be difficult; they may suck. But you have to get through those three months to get to the months and months and months *after* that where life's going to be so much better, and you're going to realize your full potential. It's not going to be smooth sailing, and you may not have a bad day, you may have a bad year. But have faith in God that you will get through it; keep your spunk and your sass and know what you're going for.

I don't see things right in front of me. I see them far off in the distance. I don't focus on the crap I'm dealing with now; I see where I want to be. Otherwise I'm never going to get there.

I am a worrywart. I am anxious. I stress about stuff and overanalyze things. But I've had to find ways to manage this because overthinking kills your soul. And it just causes more and more stress. Overthinking makes things so much worse in your mind. A few years ago, Sandra Bullock gave a graduation speech at a public high school in New Orleans. She told the audience of graduates to stop worrying so much and stop stressing about the unknown because chances are 90 percent of that stuff is not going to happen, and other challenges are going to rear their ugly heads. So why drain your energy worrying about things that are never going to happen? I had to cope with overthinking when I got fired from *The Blaze*. After all, I was nervous about paying my legal bills in addition to my rent and other monthly bills. I went from having money in the bank to having none. *What is going to happen to me*? I wondered. The only way I got through it was to ask myself, *What's the worst-case scenario?* Then I imagined that, making it as bad as possible, where everything went way south and totally wrong. I had huge legal bills that I couldn't pay, *The Blaze* won their suit against me, and nobody would hire me. Then I asked myself, *If those things happen, what will I do? This is as bad as it will possibly get, so if it comes to that, how will I react?* Figure out that game plan, have that in the back of your mind, and then let it go and give it to God. Because if you've already imagined the worst-case scenario, there is nothing else you can do. You're prepared to some degree, and it's pretty unlikely that all of it is going to happen. Maybe none of it will. So let God take it from there and move on.

Trust that God has a plan for you. If you don't, he may need to shake things up to remind you.

RECENTLY IT WAS the anniversary of my infamous appearance on *The View* and I was reflecting on the previous year. Part of that experience was my ex-boyfriend Jason, whom I dated for two and a half years. Jason is the Navy SEAL I met when I came to San Diego for One America. When I moved to Dallas, we dated long-distance for a year. My career had just started taking off when he dumped me. On the phone! Yes, the phone. And believe it or not, I got back together with him after that. Then he was with me in New York on the set of *The View* and through most of the lawsuit that followed. Just before it was settled, he dumped me for the second time. On the phone. Again. After all that I'd gone through, he was breaking up with me? He was my best friend. He saw my ups and downs. I couldn't believe that forever-and-always had an expiration date. I was really upset, but I also told him, "It's not going to be today, but someday I'm going to thank you for this." With a lot of crying and praying, I realized that love is not always mutual. Sometimes the definition is loving someone who might not love you, but you love them anyway.

Despite this lesson, the anniversary of my appearance on *The View* brought up all these old feelings. I missed Jason. It had been nine months since we'd had any contact. *I made a lot of mistakes, but I think we're supposed to be together,* I thought. I texted him. His response was not what I wanted to hear: *I'm dating somebody else now.* I could feel the tears welling in my eyes and had a pit in my stomach. He'd moved on. I sat on my kitchen floor crying with my dog in my lap. Jason didn't want me. *Look at all that I'm doing. I'm at Fox and I've got over a million Instagram followers, and I'm STILL not good enough? Who is this bitch he's dating? She must be God.* That's when I had to take a deep breath and get honest with myself: he didn't want *me.*

So many negative thoughts run through your head when you've been dumped. When he started dating someone new, I couldn't help comparing myself to her, even though I knew nothing about her. Is she on TV? Does she have a million followers? Has she had the success I've had as early as I've accomplished it? It's ridiculous, but it's what ran through my mind when my heart was broken.

It's pretty gut-wrenching to admit that someone doesn't want you. However, once I thought about it, I realized this: why, for one second, should I sit there and long for someone who doesn't even want me? When you're with the person you're *supposed* to be with, you're not going to have to convince him or her to want to be with you. Yes, it hurts when your friends see your ex with another girl or for me when I texted Jason and he told me he was with someone else. But that's when you have to face facts and remember that sometimes when you're slipping into a place that God doesn't want you to go, he has to slap you in the face with something to get you to move on. Other times when you're afraid to leap, when you're just staying in your comfort zone, God has to take that away. It hurts. Sometimes it hurts badly, but you get over it. It's a powerful thing to come into your own and realize that you can love somebody even if they don't love you. And you don't have to wish bad things on them. After a lot of thinking, I realized that Jason did shape my life, but that didn't mean he was right for me. I wasn't going to be bitter and hate him (or anyone else who had done me wrong) because then he'd still be an obsession.

The lesson God is trying to teach us over and over is that our earthly concerns are only temporary. It's easy to get caught up in the moment and forget the big picture.

What good would it do to turn to bitterness and hate? There's that expression about how holding a grudge is like drinking poison and expecting the other person to die. It's not going to happen. I also had to trust that Jason was not my person and have faith that God would lead me to my person. And he did, just a few days after that call with Jason.

Now I'm with someone who gets me, who takes my stress *away* rather than adding to it. I can be me. I can be vulnerable and honest. Your partner should be somebody who makes you want to be better but—and this is super important—doesn't want to change you to *their* idea of better. I always thought relationships were hard. I always thought I'd have to change if I wanted to be in one, long term and for life. Then I met Brandon. Not only does he love and accept me for exactly who I am, but he has shown me that when you're with the right person, relationships really aren't that hard. If you're reading this and haven't found that one yet, please know he or she is out there and may be reading this same paragraph, in this

same book, thinking the same thing you are. Trust yourself. Trust your gut. Trust God's plan.

By now you've read a lot about my past relationships,
so bear with me because I have a feeling you've been
here, too. I am in love. I have found my forever person.
However, I still look back on Jason from time to time and
wonder, What if? I still have weekly dreams about him
and my first boyfriend (whom I wouldn't touch with a
ten-foot pole). I often ask myself, *If I'm in love and* have
*found my person, why in the heck do I keep having dreams
about the past and wake up thinking about* Jason *or my
first (horrible) boyfriend?* Well, I think I've figured it out.
Those are two people who truly meant something to me,
and they rejected me. So what are these dreams about?
It's unresolved feelings of abandonment and rejection that
creep back into my subconscious even though they are
largely or even entirely unrelated to my current stresses
or situation. Yeah, it sucks. Well, Jason has six-pack abs,
so dreaming about him isn't entirely repulsive but . . . you
get the idea.

Today, even though my personal life is humming along,
I still deal with rejection in my professional life, and it
gnaws away at me whether I realize it or not. The real
hate and vitriol start coming at me when I get into "feuds"
with celebrities on social media. For example, during the

partial government shutdown in January 2019, the rapper Cardi B posted an expletive-ridden Instagram video criticizing President Trump. I responded on Twitter with a snarky jab calling her a political genius and saying I'm glad the Democrats have a new spokesperson. Now, let me be clear, Cardi B has the right to express her political opinions, and I have the right to criticize them. What happened next is textbook leftist. She tweeted that she would "dog-walk me."

For those of you who are unfamiliar with this expression, "dog-walking" someone means to beat the living hell out of them. I generally don't take threats like this to heart, but take one look at Cardi's rap sheet and you'll see she's no Mother Teresa. She's been charged with two misdemeanor counts of reckless endangerment and one misdemeanor count of assault. According to the New York City Police Department, Cardi was "throwing chairs, bottles, and hookahs in the club at 3 a.m." Yeah, I'm sure she is capable of hurting me, and I acknowledged that! Beyond Cardi, my Twitter mentions were filled with liberals (with verified accounts) applauding and encouraging threats against me. One verified Twitter user even asked for a GoFundMe page for Cardi B to knock my face in and teeth out. So, if I imply that Cardi B is not a political genius, the liberals say I'm mean and offensive. If Cardi B and her followers threaten to beat me up, the liberals laugh and encourage it. No, I didn't sit in the corner and cry about it, but these threats of physical violence aren't fun to receive. In her continued Twitter ramblings, Cardi B said I couldn't see the damage that Trump was doing to the country because I'm blinded by racism. She went to the liberal route: if you can't win a political argument, call someone a racist. Let's be clear: nothing that I said to Cardi B is based on race. Nothing. It was based on the content of her argument. Her bringing race into it just shows her victimhood complex. Furthermore, she's a stripper from the Bronx who has gone on to be one of the most popular rap artists in this country. If that is what oppression looks like in America, I'm not sure she understands what oppression means.

My FAITH IN God has helped me manage not only the pain of relationships but also a lot of the negativity that comes with living in the public eye. At every turn, people have called me names. They've called me a racist. They've called me intolerant. They've called me a bigot. They've called me ugly and dumb. Yes, I'm tough and strong, but some of these names sting.

When someone writes a nasty comment on social media or makes a mean video or meme of me—which happens almost every day—I remind myself that no one hunts small deer. I know I'm making a real difference when the nasty people come out from their bunkers and attack me the most. And I know God is putting me through those experiences for a reason, to stretch me and grow me. He has a plan.

When I did a "Final Thoughts" about Beyoncé's Super Bowl halftime show, I said that it had become a way to politicize and advance the notion that black lives matter more. It wasn't about equality; it was about ramrodding an aggressive agenda down our throats and using fame and entertainment value to do so. So what was the political message there? What were they trying to convey? A salute to what? A group that used violence and intimidation to advance, not racial equality, but an overthrow of white domination? The Black Panthers were critics of Martin Luther King's *nonviolent* civil rights movement. They didn't believe in change through peace. They promoted violence instead. The Super Bowl is the most-watched event on television. It's a game that brings Americans of every color, background, and political party together, a game where black fans cheer next to white fans, a game where teammates work together as one regardless of race, a celebration of diversity rooted in a common bond. But forget that! Beyoncé didn't reference the Black Panthers to bring about some sort of positive change; she did it to get attention, to make headlines. I also told Beyoncé that white people like her music, too. White people buy her songs on iTunes, memorize her lyrics, and admire her talent and beauty. Little white girls want to be like Beyoncé just as little black girls do. But instead of recognizing that, she'd rather perpetuate the great battle of the races. I ended by saying, "Your husband was a drug dealer. For fourteen years, he sold crack cocaine. Talk about protecting black neighborhoods, start at home."

After this, her BeyHive fan group posted thousands of mean and threatening comments on social media, flooding not only *my* Instagram page but my cousin's with bees and saying they wanted to kill me, rape me, and drag me through the streets. That summer when five officers got shot in Dallas, I got a text message from an unknown number saying, "Your life doesn't matter. It should've been you instead of those innocent black people" with a smiley face. After I was vocal about NFL player Colin Kaepernick kneeling during the national anthem, my address, phone number, and parents' number were leaked and we all got death threats.

About two years ago, the editors at *GQ* magazine spent the entire day with me. I was very generous with my time and energy, and they were so nice and friendly. We had good conversations and a great photo shoot. They told me that their goal was to do a profile of me, but the result was much more of a hit piece. I was stunned and upset by the title: "Tomi Lahren and Her Toxic Brand of Right-wing Vitriol." They were blinded by their intolerance. My point is this: people call me names every single day, and I've worked so that I don't let it even scratch the surface of my ego. The reason? I know what I am, and I know what I'm not.

For those who attempt to dismiss me and my entire career by labeling me, they are trying to explain my success and take it away from me based on their limited understanding of who I am and what I believe. I stopped wasting my time trying to disprove their labels because they're going to think what they will think regardless. By constantly attempting to disprove it, all I'm doing is giving them the credibility they don't deserve. In my experience, the left has this mentality that everything someone on the right says must be vile and disgusting since it comes from someone on the right. They also feel they have a moral obligation to attack, ridicule, and label everyone on the right because they think we are inherently evil and have fewer morals. The election of Donald Trump didn't create the left's hate; it just revealed it.

BUT YOU DON'T have to have a job like mine to experience this kind of hate and name-calling from strangers. Kaitlin Bennett was a young woman who graduated from

Kent State and posted a picture of herself on Twitter holding her graduation cap and an AR-15. In the caption, she wrote: "Now that I graduated from @KentState, I can finally arm myself on campus. I should have been able to do so as a student—especially since 4 unarmed students were shot and killed by the government on campus." I didn't know her, but she messaged my producer asking to put the two of us in touch. All these people were bullying her on Twitter, saying mean things about her "ugly" curly hair, and attacking her friends on Instagram. They were calling her "outlet mall Tomi Lahren" and other names. She didn't know how to deal with it, but I get those tweets—thousands of them—every day, so I've been there, done that. Of course, I texted her immediately. I told her that every time you stand up for yourself and get a little pushback, you have that moment where it's fight or flight. I ask myself, *Am I going to fold? Is this not for me? Or am I going to carry it through and stand my ground?* By now you know that I choose to stand my ground because every time you go through a wave of this, it means that you're doing *something.*

If you're getting bullied on social media or in person, remember this: the only reason people try to cut you down is that they're threatened by you because you have such power and you have such a voice.

After all, if you weren't making an impact and doing

something important, no one would bother you. Every time they hit you over the head, it's not because you're not enough, it's that you're *too enough*. Do not give in. I promise you that they are trying to get you to be quiet because they don't like the truth that you are speaking. You can choose to believe the horrible, disgusting things they're saying and let that make you feel like crap *or* you can say, "I'm going to wear it with pride because that means I'm doing something. I'm making waves." There are people out there that no one will ever say a bad word about because they will never talk about how they *really* feel. They will always stay in their safe zone and not rock the boat so that they can have as many followers as possible. They will never step on anyone's toes. (Think about the JoJo story I told you in chapter 2.) I told Kaitlin, and I'm telling all of you, to stay the course. Do not let these people get to you. Life will not be good if you're a shell of yourself and you follow the crowd. I don't care if you're a liberal, a conservative, or not at all political: stand up for yourself.

When I said I was pro-choice on *The View*, I stood my ground on an issue that was important to me, and I lost everything for it. Or so I thought. I'm still here, better and stronger than ever.

God put me on that journey for a reason, and I wouldn't take back a moment of it because I realized how resilient I am. I was at the highest point in my career and got knocked down to my lowest. Some people can rise from the ashes, and some can become the whole fire. I think it's better to become the whole fire. After *The Blaze* disparaged me and fired me, I didn't know my next move. I didn't know what I was going to do for a living. I practically had ulcers every time I got a bill from my attorneys. And the bills kept coming and coming. But I knew I would make it because nothing can break you if you stand your ground. It will always lead you in the right direction and so will God. Don't be a sheep. Think things through yourself and don't be afraid to go against the grain. Anytime you speak out, you're going to be a target. Most people aren't brave enough or strong enough to do that. But most people don't achieve their dreams, either. So, don't be most people. Take it as a badge of honor.

Remember that no one hunts small deer. And know that God is in your corner.

ABOUT THE AUTHOR

TOMI LAHREN is a Fox News contributor and a host on the digital streaming platform Fox Nation. She is the youngest political talk show host in history. Her signature "Final Thoughts" segments exceed five hundred million views on Facebook alone. Previously, Lahren served in a communications role at Great American Alliance, hosted *Tomi* on *The Blaze*, and *On Point with Tomi Lahren* on One America News Network.